THE A WORD

Thank You!

Maciek

Niko Sadlowski

THE A WORD

Photos: Kate Soltan

Translated by: K. Dziemianko

Edited by: Fergus Grierson

Table of Contents

I dedicate this book
to my son, Maks Sadlowski.
You taught me how to be a dad and inspire me
to never stop fighting for a new day. I love you.

THE MOMENT EVERYTHING
COULD HAVE ENDED, BUT WHICH
BECAME THE BEGINNING

I can barely remember it. I am taken to an ambulance, my eyes closing and my body shivering. I feel absent and peaceful at the same time. I couldn't care less. I don't remember much – mostly darkness. People rushing around me, someone putting me into a bath...

I'm opening my eyes. Now i can see that i am lying in a hospital bed. Darkness and peace again. I can hear voices, see flashing lights on the ceiling of a hospital corridor. Darkness again. I'm trying to open my eyes. Everything is blurry, and my eyelids are so heavy.

Somehow, I manage to open my eyes. I can see hazy figures, someone holding my hand, talking to me. I'm drifting away, gone again. I am unconscious for quite a while. I can hear voices, sense the presence of people around me, and smell the typical odour of hospital. But I'm sliding away into a shady place again.

A few years on from that moment, I'm told that there were some visitors in hospital: two of my friends, who are pretty still close to me. Even after so many years we are still in touch. Thank you for being there for me.

***

I wake up a few hours later. I struggle to keep my eyes open, but i am thrown back to reality. I realise where i am: psychiatric ward in the hospital. Let me put it straight – rehab. Damn. Looks like i went a little bit too far over the past few weeks.

I feel uncomfortable. There are few beds, iron bars in the windows, and no door handles. What the hell am i doing here?

Well, let's be honest. Two weeks of hard partying, mixing a whole range of drugs and topping up with alcohol – plus a complete lack of common sense – has finally caught up with me. Months of abusing everything i can lay my hands on, and i have hit rock bottom. I am only sixteen. Shit.

There are five beds in the room. On a bed opposite mine, we have one Colonel Josef Mushroom – schizophrenic, cavalry soldier, recipient of many medals. Well, that's what he tells me when he tries to introduce himself. Actually, he is a young man of around 20, who literally lives in the ward. He has been a resident of the hospital for the past seven years. The nurses treat him almost as a flatmate. Sometimes he leaves to return to the outside world, but he is usually back very quickly – sometimes after a few hours, sometimes a few days. He gets schizophrenic attacks and soon after he is back at 'home'.

Allocated the space next to me is a guy who has been shooting crack. He has been here more than 10 times. a well-educated young man, he can't fight his addiction. Posh parents, a good university, then a good job in an international corporation – and one step too far with drugs. Skinny, barely able to walk, wry and broken. He leaves after few days, never to return. The day after his departure i am told by the nurses that he has lost his battle with addiction: found dead with signs of overdose.

In another bed, a young high school student with overreacting parents. They caught him with a joint. His high school psychologist went ballistic and made a huge thing out of it. He was just having a laugh and good time, totally unaware of his own stupidity. Probably to teach him a lesson because of his attitude and approach to the situation, his parents demanded he be sent to detox and rehab. Well, waste of time and resources. He didn't need rehab. He needed to grow up. I guess his parents preferred to waste everyone else's time instead of talking to their son and spending some time with him, rather than their busy careers. Maybe he just wanted to get their attention. It didn't work.

That was my situation around the ages of 15 and 16. I don't mention this because i want to show how badly i started out. All the decisions in my life were made by me. I was in many dark places in my youth, and it took nearly 20 years to confront these memories for the first time. I'm also reminded of my suicide attempt. Flashbacks of the past came to me some time ago, when i was watching a YouTube video about a young man with mental illness who decided to jump off the Golden Gate Bridge. He is one of the few people to have made the attempt and survive.

I have two unsuccessful suicide attempts behind me. One attempt with meds, and the second with a belt. I am really ashamed. I don't know if i was desperate or screaming for help. Maybe i was also just looking for attention. I feel very lucky i didn't take the time to think it through. Even today, I get goose-pimples thinking about those moments. But i can live with it. I never told anyone about it, and life goes on. I have moved on.

I'm writing about it because by the end of this book, it should be possible to understand something. I want to show that you and i – all of us – have a journey to complete. Everything depends on actions we take. I started my journey from a dark swamp – but i managed to make it through until i found a sandy beach. I have never had any regrets, even when things turned bad. Of course, I would love to have avoided some situations in my life, and have done things differently, but we can't turn back time. You can't fix the world in your head.

Try to start from one thing: stop for a moment, look around and move forward for a better tomorrow. Pathetic bullshit? Maybe, but look at me – fate throws different issues at us, and we have to find a way to avoid or resolve them – or learn how to live with it.

WHERE TO START?

Dear son. I'm watching you running around full of excitement, humming and squeezing your chin. You see the world in your own way. Until the end of my days, I will wonder how you perceive the world around you. How do you see light? What do you hear? How is your perception of the universe different from mine? You're seven years old, but my knowledge about you is insignificant. You surprise me every day. Nothing in your world is constant, but some things are stable – at least temporarily. I never know for how long.

Autism. a short word which contains more than a whole encyclopaedia. a word which squeezes out tears from the toughest lads. a word that changes people, that changed me, your mother and the way we live today. a word that creates fear and so many conflicted feelings. a diagnosis that combines the emotions and the journey of a single human being, always creating a different picture every time.

How do i see autism? As though through fog, I can feel it in the air. First of all, I see you, my son. In the same way we are talk about race, gender or unusual looks, I would love to believe that after your diagnosis, society will see a human being first. But nothing has such a great impact on us as disability – any disability. When we meet someone for the first time, how many times do we see the disability and not the person? How often do we think about individual characters, rather than labels, which in fact do not define us?

Let's come back to you, my son. You're a seven-year-old nonverbal child, with (according to assessment) a learning disability. You have been diagnosed with autism. I would love to tell you so many things. The scariest thing for me is that you can't tell me if you're in pain, uncomfortable or just sad. I can't stand it.

THE DAY WHEN TIME STOPPED
FOR THE FIRST TIME

You were a toddler. a little bit after your first birthday, you were starting walk around the house, interested in everything. Your sister wasn't born yet, but maybe once in a while we'd mentioned that it would be nice to have a sibling for you. I can remember you trying to reach us from your cot, shouting *"Mummy! Daddy!"*. I can still remember the cheerful sound of your voice. My Maks… I remember when you had colic and i had to move your tiny feet slowly to make you fall asleep.

I think about this particular day now only very rarely. There's no point. We were afraid about the possible link between the MMR vaccination and autism, so we had postponed it. And on this day, you woke up with a severely runny nose and cough. Something disturbing was happening. a routine GP check – some kind of infection. Nothing major, but serious enough to prescribe antibiotics.

Yet after two days, you developed a serious mouth infection. a high fever and crying. Gums so swollen we could barely see your teeth. You were so hungry, but every single time we tried to give you milk, you refused. In pain, you would throw your bottle away. We didn't know how to help you. The doctor said it would pass within three days, but they were the longest three days of our lives.

We made another GP visit, were given different antibiotics, and finally saw some progress. Your appetite returned, and the swelling disappeared – but the Maks we knew disappeared with it.

***

You stopped talking. From that day on, we never again heard the word "*mum*" spontaneously. I remember you standing in your cot. The light and spark in your eyes from before the infection was gone. Today i know that at this very moment you became autistic, and that the infection had worked as the trigger to activate it. I don't want to get involved in medical theories – this is my side of the story and this is how i see what happened. Dear son – this was the day i watched you leaving. I didn't realise it back then, but today i know that your empty gaze was the beginning of everything. Your smile disappeared. I saw it – autism taking you away from me.

I believe that one day we will reclaim you, in good shape, capable of reading these memories of mine. This day, I started a small battle which led to a huge war. One day, we will win this war together.

***

It was a difficult moment. I need to add that you stopped developing and reaching your milestones for a year. Actually, it's more accurate to say that you regressed and stopped. I only found out for sure when they handed over official diagnosis papers 18 months later. But with the passage of time i can join the dots and know: this was the day my son became autistic. Silence and tears. An ocean of tears to be precise.

WHAT SORT OF FEELINGS
CAN YOU EXPERIENCE?

I call myself a rock n roll person and can be sharp tongued when i need to be. Living away from my own country has led to my carrying a few extra pounds of life experience. a new place means new people, and the ability to start again. I'm not one for giving advice, and we are all different. Everyone has to find their own way. For each person, a diagnosis or even a suspicion of autism is an incomparable and totally personal experience. I want to convey how this might feel. Provide a manual. Working title: *"It's OK to Feel Like This When Your World is Crashing Down"*. So, it is OK to be totally pissed off – and this is exactly how i felt when the word 'autism' first showed up in our family home.

The first time someone suggested that Maks wasn't right – some nice lady had said that he might be autistic – we felt that our world had been blown up into tiny pieces. I wondered what was going on, and how it could be possible. How could someone meeting our son for just the second time ever say such a thing? I was angry that someone could lob in such an insult so light heartedly – just like that. By the evening i was exhausted. My head was spinning, and my mind was scrambled. At the time, I thought the best solution was to go to the pub and have a few shots.

Under such circumstances, it's natural to feel small, helpless, and cheated. I was self-centred enough to shout out loud, *"why us?!"* To this day this question is still on my lips, but with time i have learned to swap it for: *"what now?"* and *"what's next?"*. To move forward and leave these feelings behind.

It's also natural to feel resentment when parents of neurotypical children try to tell you how to raise an autistic son. They give you tips suggesting what to do when they have no clue what they are talking about, and you have just one wish – to chop their heads off with a spade. Don't be afraid – this too will pass. In time, you will smile again and proudly respond to their advice. If you can know they don't mean any harm, you can turn it into loud laughter.

It will become natural for your sexual relationship to be replaced by long nights of talking and trying to cheer up your partner. It might actually take a year or more to notice, but you will not mind. Friends will accuse you of talking only about autism, tests, diagnosis, and appointments, and within six months they will stop asking you to come out with them for a pint. They will hold a grudge and say that it's impossible to talk to you anymore. Don't worry, it will pass.

No-one needs to be around unsupportive people in difficult moments, or those that run away like rats from a sinking ship, blaming you for steering them into the iceberg called autism.

GRIEF

After an autism diagnosis, grief is a big, very healthy and natural thing. Psychologists and psychiatrists write about how such grief is comparable to losing a child. And I'm not talking about death, but of parents losing the child they'd always imagined. Each of us needs to deal with it in our own way, and it can be especially hard for mothers, after carrying a child for so long. It took my wife years to come to terms with it, to accept it and to move on.

I managed to deal with it quite fast, more or less within a year. To survive, I had to have a carrot in front of me – actually a bucket of carrots – and i took on a number of different projects. My first and main mission was to support my wife and be a father of two. I went to college to study early education and childcare. I started working with autistic adults and got into self-development and coaching. I also attended all appointments and autism-related training as my son's assistant. I started getting up at five am, jogging ten kilometres a day and visiting the gym. I went to college until three or four pm, squeezing in family time and then spending my evenings on self-development. In between, I took driving lessons. I had to do so many things to keep myself busy, so i wouldn't feel down. There were many times i cried while taking a shower or sitting on the bus. Each small step made me feel so emotional. My life had turned into a cycle, and i realised that my way of dealing with it all was to be busy. But when i was done with college, had passed my driving test, and lost few kilos it turned out that there was now plenty of time, and the sadness finally got me.

***

When it comes to diagnosis and going through all the tests, interviews and meetings, you can feel like the one who has had autism injected into your body. Looking at your child can feel like experiencing an autopsy on a live organism. Seeing clearly all the changes and abnormalities, you come to understand the reality. You watch and analyse the behaviour of a small autistic child, and in the end, you finally get it – the world is not fair. And the grief comes pouring out.

Sometimes i think it is good that our son unaware of his situation and can't feel what we have to go through as we meet with the stigma of autism in society.

IT HURTS MOST THE FIRST TIME

I remember walking down the street as a family. I was holding Maks' hand, and my wife was pushing our daughter Livia in a buggy. We ran into some people we'd met at a restaurant we'd visited some time before. They knew that Maks was autistic, but with them was someone we didn't know, a lad with a moustache who we'll call Fred.

Fred wanted to be a good 'uncle' and tried to get Maks to give him a high five, but Maks wasn't interested. Our son is far from shy, but there was no eye contact. After trying to convince Maks to respond, I felt had to say something as Fred looked a bit confused. "Don't worry," I said, "Maks is autistic. That's why he's not responding." And at this moment lightning struck my heart. Fred replied: "He's autistic? He doesn't look like it."

A small thing, but also something you should never say to parents of a child with autism. I know that people have the best intentions, and that they want to reassure us that that our kids seem normal, but it's really not helpful. I have an old friend who lives in Belgium. Her four-year-old daughter is fighting cancer and sometimes she hears the same thing. "Did she have chemo? She doesn't look like it". People are trying to be nice and cheer us up, and i understand why. But sometimes it's better to shut up.

I can tell you how i felt on this occasion. I remember feeling knocked down, like someone slapped me in the face, my heart pierced with sadness. But i just kept my mouth shut and smiled through gritted teeth. Inside, I wanted to shout out: "You're an ignorant and idiot, but it doesn't look like it", but instead, I smiled nicely and said "bye". We walked off in silence, with Maks jumping and enjoying our walk.

But i was angry, helpless, scared, and ashamed – ashamed because i couldn't cope. Believe me, it was hard to deal with. Only later was i able to start a conversation again with my wife. I just nodded and said, "Well, Maks doesn't look like it, eh? Fred doesn't look ignorant either, but…" We both laughed, and i stroked our boy's innocent head.

Unfortunately, you will feel like this more than once. You will expect the world to be aware and have some familiarity with autism, but it seems that society's knowledge about autism spectrum disorder (ASD) is minimal. With time, you will learn what to say, in one short sentence, when someone asks what's wrong with your child: "Never fucking ending story."

At this point, an idea about how to turn this kind of situation around began to form in my mind. From then on, I decided to start every conversation with someone i had just met by stating: "Hi, my name is Niko. I am married, and we have two kids. Our son is autistic and nonverbal, and our daughter is neurotypical." Just to be honest and open about it. And i wonder why i now have so few friends!

But seriously – this short piece of information could be just enough to avoid awkwardness around new people. It might be a bit over the top, but it could also help to raise awareness, since many people i meet admit to associating different stereotypes with autism in children.

What can you do? Be an autism ambassador. This is the best thing you can do. Try to change the stereotypes. This strategy can be used for every disability, sickness, mental health issue, or taboo subject. Don't settle for labels, or negative attitudes people take towards these issues. Today, I'm a "walking autism fighter". I even have tattoos about autism. Be proud. It's not easy to build this frame of mind but it is important to try. No one would claim that it is easy, but it is worth the effort.

THE WORLD IN PIECES

Let's go back to that day when the sky cracked open. Our sky. It was a cosy life: work, a flat, a little daughter and our wee boy. We were living in London, and we had taken them to a local playgroup. I was playing with Maks, and Ewa was having a coffee and chat with some of the other mums while Livia was having a nap. The playgroup was like many others in the UK, and we had been visiting this one regularly. Usually, I was the only man present as i was working mainly back shifts in catering. But, I had time with my children, and i loved it.

One day after playgroup, one of the mums came up and asked straight out if we considered the possibility that Maks could be autistic. She went on to state that she thought he might be, because he demonstrated typical autistic behaviour. Boom!

On our way home later, my wife was telling me about this unusual chat, and i just walked, analysing her words. I felt discomfort and uncertainty, and minutes later, I broke into tears. I knew that things were not right, but i couldn't believe that someone had the guts to suggest something like that straight to our faces. It was like being punched, but things were only getting started.

Today i know that what she said was wrong. As an early years practitioner, I have no right to throw my opinion around and put someone in this sort of position. No one should. When i look back, I remember how my sadness turned onto anger. I asked myself "*How could she*?" It's the kind of thing that can only be known after rounds of referral, procedure, and observation, especially in well-educated countries.

I could not pick myself up after that day. When the children finally went to sleep i opened a bottle of whiskey. I sat down in silence in our garden and i got drunk. Each of us has our own way of processing things. I'm not ashamed. Drinking and crying, I looked up and i knew that life would never be the same. Now, as i relate this story i feel less emotional. I see other things as much more important. Does it still hurt? Who knows? I don't think so. I have got used to the sky being cracked open, and my heart bleeding.

THE NEXT STEP

What happened after? How did we manage to live our lives after such dramatic realisation?

I was looking at my son sitting on the floor, happily playing with his toys. The world he knew didn't change, but my world did. Our world did. I'm writing things from my own perspective, but i hope one day my wife will tell her side of this story. a mother's view.

I started by browsing the internet, searching for information about diagnostic procedures and about the steps we should take.

In Poland, we use the word *therapy* in the context of autism. Over here, the word *therapy* is not so connected. The word used more often is *education* – that is, dealing with the condition by working on different sets of skills.

But, let's get back to the subject. After visiting our GP, we found out that the waiting list to get diagnosed in London might be long – even as long as two years. I tried to understand it, but i couldn't. Two precious years wasted. It was just too much.

MOVING ON

I decided we should move. After a long talk with my wife, we decided to leave London. She wasn't happy about it, but she didn't reject the idea either. I wanted to move to Scotland. I had been in Edinburgh a few years before, and i loved it. I also had a mate there who offered me a place to crash until i could get everything sorted out.

I rented a truck and some storage space in Edinburgh, then bought tickets to Poland for my wife and kids and sent them away for few weeks. In Poland, Maks got a fast-track diagnosis thanks to a friend. December passed quickly. I was picking up bits of work in Edinburgh, and in January i landed a permanent position. Soon after, I found a decent flat and got my family back with me. Mission accomplished.

DIAGNOSIS BACK AT HOME

We had managed to pick ourselves up after the realisation that Maks might be autistic but being apart from each other was like being knocked down all over again. Getting the results of the assessment in Poland would be the third heavy blow we would face after the word autism became part of our lives.

> *"Developmental problems fit within autism areas. His speech is impaired, and abnormalities are not compensated with other non-verbal communication such as mimic or gesture. Development of social skills is also qualitatively and quantitatively impaired. Play and spontaneous activity are very poor and schematic.*
>
> *"Maks is able to say a few single words, but communicates using a parent's hand, guiding them in the direction of a wanted object. Sometimes we are able to hear word "give". Sometimes he responds to his own name. He does not answer to complex commands and does not share objects of interest with adults. Contact with Maks is very limited. He does not initiate contact except when he feels that he needs something.*
>
> *"With very little interest in cooperation during play, he does not participate in activities. Eye contact is also very poor, not containing common elements of reciprocity. Maks is also not interested in playing with*

other children. Spontaneous activity is additionally very limited, with a poor range of behaviours.

"Maksymilian's individual play is far more stimulated, utilising some elements of thematic play, but these are very limited in scope. Due to observed impairments across the areas mentioned, he is in need of intensive, multi-specialist therapy. We also recommend support in early years development and in small group preschool therapy. Maks's parent has been informed about diagnosis and the next steps."

Boom! Life in pieces. I saw it in this way, and i assumed that my life was ruined. It was difficult and painful and took us a long time to shake off and get over. I was sent a scan of the assessment and i read it over and over. It felt like the diagnosis of someone else's child, not ours. My wife called later that afternoon and she sobbed on the phone. It took me weeks to accept it, but with time passing i came to understand what was written there.

As a parent trying to manage autism, you might be keen on being idealistic, putting a positive spin on things, or viewing things through rose-tinted glasses. But with everything set down in black and white, there's nowhere to hide. Put simply, a written diagnosis will bring you crashing down to earth no matter what. Old wounds open up again. How is it that something like this can happen when you don't deserve any of it?

I locked myself in my flat and i cried the whole weekend. I had some cigarettes and i smoked them. Did i mention that i am a non-smoker? I was done, I was alone, and i didn't want anyone to see me in such a state.

If you've felt similar, don't be ashamed. To roughly translate a line from a Polish song, "*sometimes i cry because i need to; I feel all evil leaving from inside me*". I woke up on the Sunday feeling less heavy, my soul cleaner and lighter. Three years on, I haven't smoked in my flat since.

CLOSED DOORS

Over the next couple of weeks, I decided it would be good time to start sorting out Maks' education, so i started calling and emailing relevant charities, organisations and associations. We needed information and help about the disability living allowance (DLA) and everything else what could be beneficial for Maks, and us as his family.

There was a surprise waiting for us – every single person i spoke to asked if Maks had been diagnosed in the UK. Obviously, the answer was no, since Maks had gone through the process in Poland. Unfortunately, due to this small detail, I was asked to call or email again when we had confirmed the autism diagnosis over here.

Honestly? I was pissed off. Each person passing me on to someone else, from one institution on to another. Phone calls directed to other phone numbers. The gauntlet had been thrown down, and there was only one solution – we needed to translate Maks' diagnosis and go to a GP with him as soon as my family arrived back in Edinburgh. It was a good call. On the 5th of March, my family was back with me, and in June Maks had his diagnosis confirmed by the NHS. Guess what happened next? We started to open up old wounds...

For my wife it was a new situation. She was on her own with two kids, without any friends around, while i had to work long hours. I can imagine how difficult it was for her, and today i can only say how proud i am of her! I always have been. That woman has some balls; she was able to handle all of it, even when i was burnt out.

I hated my job and i didn't have anyone close to me in the UK, and these issues started to be a massive burden. I was worried about my children. I wanted a real home for them, away from autism and all those meetings with specialists. Each of them needed a different type of Dad, and i wanted to be the father they deserved. How could i provide them the stability they needed? How could i give the kind of parenting essential for the happiness and development of one of them without hurting the other?

I couldn't create a home in the shadow of autism. Maks was constantly irritated and nervous. He wasn't really keen on taking *"no"* for an answer. There was a lot of shouting, screaming and crying under our roof.

COMING OUT OF DIAGNOSIS

So many words were said to us, a lot of things were explained in detail, and i managed to research a lot myself. The worst moment of all was saying *"goodbye"* after leaving the GP's office before the next time. That was the case with us. Closing the doors behind me and walking away holding my child's hand. The corridor seemed so long, like an escalator moving in the opposite direction, going backwards instead of forwards. Billions of thoughts in my head and my heart – silent tears and complete sadness.

It's one of those moments you don't fully realise how bad things are, but you can feel your heart bleeding. Your child is walking by your side, holding your hand, so cheerful and happy, and you know that you can't get to his world. I recall someone passing by, giving us a smile...

There is a scene in the Keanu Reeves film *Constantine*, where the main character walks along a path through hell, with fire and destruction all around him. I could imagine us walking like that into nowhere, with the sadness of every poor soul upon me.

It took probably a minute or two to leave the medical centre, but it felt like forever. Hearing a buzzing noise in my ears, unable to stop my thoughts banging around inside my head, my heart bleeding. On one hand i wanted to stop and scream, and on the other i wanted to leave that place as quickly as possible and never come back.

We were walking in complete silence. Maks was so peaceful, and i could see contemplation in his eyes. He seemed to see the world in a different way, like he was learning from all the knocks as an autistic child, not like a strange child without a diagnosis.

From this moment we could put a label on us, on Maks. The 'A' word – *autism* – became our companion for the rest of our lives. Don't get me wrong, it's not about defining our child by the word autism. You will see in the rest of the book how i am always saying that it's not autism that defines who we are; autistic people are extraordinary, and they are individual characters.

What changed was that now we finally knew what was wrong with Maks. We had this magical piece of paper, a name, certainty. There was no more guessing, no place for insecurity. We had a diagnosis, an unbelievable amount of sadness, but relief as well. All of it mixed with the big question, *"why us?"*. Why did fate choose us for this test? There was comfort in knowing what was happening with our boy, but there was also the question of what was going to happen in the future, and what our life would look like – of *what next?!*

With your world on fire, you feel like you don't need or want anyone. I stopped on the pavement, crouched down and hugged my son. *"It's going to be ok my son,"* I said, repeating, *"Everything will be fine, I promise you..."*

WHAT IS AUTISM?

I would like to explain how i see autism. I don't want to go too deep into medical terminology; the internet is full of smart words and explanations, even though the average person has minimal knowledge about autism.

Autism is a disability. It is not an illness as some might think – there is no cure for it. It is primarily caused by changes in the brain. Genetics play a massive part, but there are no clear-cut grounds for telling exactly what causes it, and what can trigger it. What is interesting is that it is mostly diagnosed in boys – currently, statistics say the ratio is 4:1, meaning that for every four autistic boys, only one girl is diagnosed.

In 1979 two researchers, Lorna Wing and Judith Gould, presented a theory regarding the 'triad of impairments'. Very often, autistic people have problems with the development of certain elements of personality connected with three aspects of their life. In autistic people, impairments can appear in reciprocal social interaction, in reciprocal communication, and in the scope and range of their interests and activities.

We need to remember – every autistic person is different, even when we can observe common characteristics like in every group of people.

Social interaction impairment can come in different forms and can be reflected on different levels. We might meet a non-verbal ASD person who can communicate via computer software, using the picture exchange communication system (PECS) or sign language. At the same time, we might come across someone who cannot talk at all and does not show any need or interest in communication skills or in contact with the outside world. I also know of people affected by autism who are able to run a conversation smoothly, express their needs, and share their knowledge eloquently and very intelligently.

With regard to social interaction, we can observe a lack of understanding of generally accepted rules of interpersonal contact, a lack of ability to judge situations, and an inability to recognise the feelings and emotions of others.

Some of the autistic people with whom i have had an opportunity to work don't understand why they are not allowed to greet and hug every single person on the street if everyone else they're with is doing so. It's a classic example that shows the absence of being able to assess a situation and other people's feelings – as well as the inability to read facial expressions and the meaning of gestures in neuro-typical people.

Another element of the image of an autistic person is imagination, which most neuro-typical people are gifted with. Noticeable in the case of people with autism is the inhibition or impairment of behavioural flexibility and imaginative thinking, as well as problems with understanding metaphor, sarcasm, and irony. We can add to this troubles with tracking time, and the incorrect perception of other non-physical factors. Difficulties with recognising other people's feelings may appear as well.

These are characteristics of every autistic person. Now, imagine that you have two levers. Better still – try to visualize three sliders in a TV or recording studio. Each of them can be moved through any position from one to ten. If we assume that those sliders can describe the situation of a particular autistic person, all of them can be placed on a different value.

If we take my son, for example, the first slider responsible for communication might be pushed to five. He can't communicate with the outside world by using the methods we usually use. He can't hold a conversation with another human being, but he can express his emotions by quoting sentences from cartoons. When he is upset with something, he says: *"you're a toy!"*, like Woody from *Toy Story*, using the same facial expression as the character. In addition to speech, he can pull my sleeve and show me what he wants, and he uses his fingers, images and many other things.

Now the second slider – an indicator of social interaction skills. In Maks' case, it would show three, meaning a lack of contact with others. He is not interested in other children and i would even say that he tries to avoid contact with them as they tend to be unpredictable. He is more likely to pay attention to adults, but that also happens only very rarely. He is not aware of any dangers or the existence of social norms. He could easily run off in a random direction because he is not aware of possible risks on the road, and he doesn't know that he might get lost and we will not be able to find him. Better still, he will not have a clue that he is lost.

He doesn't know that we all have to follow some rules, and he does not use common sense. At this stage, for example, he is not able to understand that he shouldn't take a toy from a shop just because he likes it. I could go on to list a million other areas of his development in which he has deficiencies but hopefully, the reasons why Maks needs to be under the constant supervision of an adult can be imagined and understood. For him, the outside world is a great danger.

At this point, I would like to highlight that autistic children have the potential learn a lot of things. Maks is just six years old, so i am confident that with time he will understand social interaction skills better. We can't take it for granted, but we will fight to make it happen until he does.

Maks' slider for imagination and thinking flexibility hasn't been used very much so far. Since there is no way to check if Maks' imaginative thinking is affected by autism, we could say that we are not sure which level it shows. As i write this book, I would place this slider on five, simply because he uses quotes from cartoons in particular situations. This is a fact which confirms that in Maks' case, imagination works pretty well. As well as the emotion he shows and the progress he has made through contact with us and alternative forms of communication, the indication is that he is using his imagination on a daily basis. For the time being, however, it is hard to confirm this exactly because the levels of his language and social interactions are very low.

I know people with all sliders on level zero – a complete absence of verbal and non-verbal communication skills, no sign of understanding the common rules of the regular world, and without any means to check how their imagination works. To these factors, we can add a heavily affected sense of time – what counts is the here and now, a factor which can be only solved by keeping each day's tasks appropriately and consistently organised. In this, a routine has to be introduced to every aspect of their lives to guarantee the maximum amount of calm and minimise the fear of change.

An autistic person can be taught many things, but this depends on how quickly we start their education, what sort of methods we use and which doors to their mind we can open. Very often, what works for one person doesn't work for another, or can even cause more harm. It's a big lottery and requires a massive amount of luck. Patience and knowledge are very often the keys to success.

MAKS... OH MY DEAR MAKS

Where should i start? You are an extraordinary fighter. I look at you every day and i can't believe how many battles you have already won. It amazes me how much willpower you have. Still in nappies when you were four and a half years old, it didn't look like you were anywhere close to being ready or able to move on. For over two years we wondered how we might be able to get you to use the toilet. When we tried potty training, you cried and screamed like you had been skinned alive. The bathroom and toilet were so terrifying for you that you would get muscle contractions and spasms at the slightest mention of them.

Remember, every autistic person is different. You see, you decided one day that you didn't want to wear a nappy anymore. You didn't let me put a fresh one on, and we were worried, but we put your pants on without one anyway. I still recall how proud you were, staring at the little picture on the front of them. You peed yourself – once – and that was the last time it happened! We went to the bathroom, changed your clothes, and from then on you went to the toilet on your own. I never stop wondering how many moments like that we will have together... Loads, I bet.

Dear parent, if the mussel doesn't open, don't eat it. Autistic kids very often need more time and space to make connections in their own way. Sometimes too much pressure works opposite to what we want to achieve. Let your child discover the world on their own terms and at their own pace. You should provide support and let them feel that everything is OK. Don't push, and don't force anything.

EATING

My dear boy! How is it that you're not anaemic, and your blood test results come back in perfect order? I have no clue, and probably nobody knows.

Your diet consists of very few things: toast with jam, dry baked rolls, rolls with Nutella or cheese, and chicken nuggets. Sometimes you go for an apple, massive amounts of strawberries or grapes. Pizza, and literally anything from McDonald's. Instant noodles and cookies. All kinds of sweets and candies. Juices and eggs – but *only* runny eggs! Only!

Dear parent, always remember that if your son's cookie breaks in half, it will be a tragedy very close to the apocalypse. If the ketchup 'broke the rules' and stained the plate in the wrong place, if the egg is hanging from the spoon in an asymmetrical way or the burger from McDonald's has a pickle inside, you have no chance of success. Chicken nuggets or burger meat needs to be cut into pieces exactly the same size, and you need to take all the green veggies and spices or herbs out of the soup.

I need to mention that if by any chance Maks stains his shirt or any piece of clothing while eating, it means the end of eating. We will have a meltdown, and without a doubt – because the stain will be toxic or acidic and can damage fabric and skin – his clothes will need to be changed in less than three seconds and be washed straight away. Plus, it's such a disgrace that it has to be announced to the entire neighbourhood.

One day, one of our neighbours popped in for a chat with your mother. After some time spent gossiping, she was just about to leave when you ran through the hallway fully dressed.

The conversation continued for maybe two minutes and out of nowhere, you appeared completely naked. Our neighbour was so surprised that she almost wet herself laughing. For us, it was a normal reality. Our reality.

Whenever we go out for dinner or visit friends we always take a full backpack of clothes. Just in case. It's normal, only one of many things happening on a daily basis. Just one! There are hundreds, maybe even thousands of other little things like that. We learn them together every day.

Those are the colours of autism. For you, it might be the end of the world. For us, they are tiny doors to your world, opening up to reveal a little bit of mystery. This will probably sound a bit like overreaction or exaggeration, but it's not. You can never understand it until you have an autistic person permanently in your life.

TROUBLE WITH DIGESTION

There are many concepts associated with autism and diet. Some of us believe in gluten-free food, and that our stomach and guts are connected with the brain, so that incorrect dietary choices can block brain activity. Others are convinced that limiting sugars and replacing them with stevia and xylitol hold the keys to a miracle.

The biggest problem we had with Maks was not in fact with food and diet itself, but with excreting. It's a pretty common problem with autistic kids – at the age of three, Maks had terrible constipation. Unfortunately, with Maks' very limited choice of food and his aversion to change, we have been forced to try almost everything. Normally, our son was pooping every 10 to 14 days, but the record was 23 days. Every two to three weeks! Can you imagine that? I don't think i need to explain the sort of pain and agony involved, and we were right there with him.

With time, another problem occurred – Maks developed a fear of going to the toilet, as he began to associate the pain felt while defecating with the process itself. After a week without going – stopping himself from doing it – he was barely eating at all, just drinking water and lying on the floor in agony, kicking around to somehow stop the pain. He couldn't play or go to the playground because the contractions in his intestines were causing extreme pain. The stool stopping up his guts grew to the size of a fist, and the cramps caused by it bearing down inside were unbelievable. Maks cried – I would even call it howling and yelling – and we did as well.

We tried everything: massaging his belly, administering lactulose, and sneaking pills into drinks. Our GP prescribed paraffin oil. I felt like i was giving my son some sort of fuel to drink. I even got to the point where i ordered some water from magical caves in Australia, which apparently had a high volume of minerals. I didn't have anything to lose except money. a pint of Australian water cost me about £70. Who wouldn't try it, if there was at least a small chance that it might stop your child from suffering? We tried everything.

Obviously, it didn't help. After so many months, Maks' body was poisoned. His skin was really pale, almost transparent, and his eyes were circled. He became a very sad and unhappy child. Needless to say, his development ground to a halt, and he stopped answering our questions – his entire attention and focus was on fighting the pain and agony of his body. In the morning he would wake up in tears, then go to nursery and just sit on the floor fighting his constipation. After getting back home, things were exactly the same. His stool was causing bleeding and was so hard after coming out that i couldn't even crush it in my hand. a nice, funny topic, don't you think? However, I want you to realise that autism is paired with many abnormalities and malfunctions.

We started to give him yogurts; probiotics, obviously. That didn't change much either. One day, my wife found some sort of strawberry-flavoured probiotic tablets in a shop with health food and diet supplements. Maks was really happy to try them, and finally his intestines started to work. He was going to the toilet more often, and there was less pain involved. After two weeks, more or less, everything got back in order. By the time he was five, the bacterial flora in his gut had rebuilt and normalised itself, and our boy was back to full health. Now he doesn't even need the probiotic, and everything is in good order. We can finally breathe with relief.

Maks moved forward and he changed a lot. He put on weight. Autistic children have very specific metabolisms, and despite a very limited diet, his body is somehow able to gather the necessary minerals and vitamins. That's our brave fighter.

COMPULSIVE BEHAVIOUR

In this case, we are really lucky because Maks doesn't have many of them. They come, and they go away. Autistic children very often get bonded to certain items and consistent rituals, and every change causes their world to fall apart.

When Maks was much younger, he didn't leave home without his favourite toy, Bunny. He took it everywhere he went. Some of the children i know or have worked with need to go to nursery or school in exactly the same way – always taking one certain thing with them; a piece of clothing, a bottle cup or a DVD. Not having it would be the end of the world. It's interesting how the human brain can need 'comforting' items – something to calm down, soothe fears and lower levels of unpredictability.

Most people sometimes encounter difficult times in between moments of everyday struggle. I look at Maks, and for him the possible end of the world lurks behind every corner. His world can collapse at any point. That makes me realise that our problems are tiny; like dust.

Milestone number 168: I am seating on my sofa, we're playing with kinetic sand. You are covering a toy car with it, trying to bury it completely. Livia is playing next to us. I love the moments when we find something what we can all do together, and you are interested in it as well.

"Daddy," Livia shouts. "Yes, darling?"

"Maks is different." I smile at her. "I am different as well! And mummy, and you! We're all different!"

"Yes, sweetheart," I answer with a smile.

From around a year old, since she was big enough to understand, I've been trying to explain to Livia that her brother is a little bit different than other people. We talk a lot. I would like our daughter to know what is happening with her brother. I want her to have her own image of autism and understand from an early age what disability means. She already started to talk in sign language with her granny on Skype.

If we show our kids what disability is, and we educate them in the correct way, being different will not be anything extraordinary, like the fact that my parents were deaf for me. Children do not judge – they accept. Sometimes they can be brutally honest, but that's a part of discovering the world. I wonder if we adults shouldn't be a little bit more like kids.

LANGUAGE

For now, Maks is a nonverbal autistic boy. One thing that needs to be understood, my dear reader, is that being non-verbal doesn't always mean not talking at all. Maks is capable of quoting most of the movie or the cartoon he has watched or of singing an entire song or repeating phrases he has overheard somewhere and remembered.

He just doesn't have a need for a communication. Only if he really, really wants something is he motivated to engage in contact with the outside world.

During the last meeting at school we spoke with Maks' teachers about how much he had achieved so far, and what sort of steps we should take to focus on developing his verbal skills. In class, he uses the picture exchange communication system (PECS) – a board with a wide range of pictures on velcro which start from *"I want..."* or *"I see..."*

We gave Maks his own pictures of everyday items and places to use. My wife i and are both Polish, but we communicate with Maks in English, mostly because of school and for the benefit of his development. If Maks wants to say something, he needs to take one of the pictures and stick it on the board as a beginning, for example, *"I want..."*, followed by with a picture of a glass, for instance. He then needs to present all the pictures either to his teacher or to us and point out each word with his finger while saying, "I want a drink". Only after doing all of this will he get what he wants.

Every month he has been doing much better, and the selection of pictures is growing and growing. Maybe it does sound difficult and complicated, but it's the only way he can understand that communication is necessary.

Maks, like many autistic children, thinks that we know his thoughts. He assumes that if he thinks about something we will instantly know about it. Every parent of a child with ASD has to accept this.

A concept known as the *theory of mind* (ToM) suggests why autistic children don't see the same differences as neurotypical children.

> *"Research on theory of mind, in humans and animals, adults and children, normally and atypically developing, has grown rapidly in the 35 years since Premack and Guy Woodruff's paper, 'Does the chimpanzee have a theory of mind?'.[1] The emerging field of social neuroscience has also begun to address this debate, by imaging the brains of humans while they perform tasks demanding the understanding of an intention, belief or other mental state in others.*
>
> *"An alternative account of theory of mind is given within operant psychology and provides significant empirical evidence for a functional account of both perspective-taking and empathy. The most developed operant approach is founded on research on derived relational responding and is subsumed within what is called* relational frame theory.
>
> *"According to this view, empathy and perspective-taking comprise a complex set of derived relational*

abilities based on learning to discriminate and respond verbally to ever more complex relations between self, others, place, and time, and through established relations."

Put succinctly, when our autistic child thinks about a certain item or action, they automatically assume we already know what he or she is thinking about, or what they desire. They see the world in their own way and their brain speculates that we see exactly the same things and we feel everything the way they do.

Here comes the break with reality! They ask themselves *"why don't they understand what i want?"*, or, *"why don't others see that I'm sad and angry?"* It's heart-breaking, but unfortunately, it's real. Those things which for us are obvious are beyond understanding for ASD children. Their brains simply work and operate in a distinct way.

IT'S TOUGH FOR ME

I am wondering how to break the tension in you. Every time you hear *"stop", "don't throw that", "please, pick it up,"* or *"come over here"*, your reaction is equal to the arrival of Armageddon. I am here with you and for you, but please my dear son, help me with this fight!

You know what the saddest thing is? That i have no idea why you're behaving this way. I don't know how to get to the bottom of the problem, and even when i follow all the clues, I get lost. Is it because you're trying to be independent and you don't like other people telling you what to do? Is it your age? Maybe it's just one of the passing stages of development?

I've tried changing and modulating my tone of voice to make it sound more friendly, funny, scary or pleading, but the reaction is always the same – nothing. Is there you're something trying to tell me, or are you just irritated?

One night you came to our bedroom and lay down next to me. Your eyes were wet with tears, your face was pouting, and you grabbed my hand. When you asked me to place my index finger in your right ear, I knew straight away that you were in pain. I know you very well.

Your mum brought some painkilling syrup and eardrops. The next day, the doctor told us you had an ear infection. Now we knew what the problem was, all of the scenes, moods and irritability had a real source. Most likely you had been feeling bad for a couple of days. There are times when i can't help you and i would really like to, without any delay or hesitation. It's so tough!

That's how life is with a non-verbal child. Very often i would give almost everything to swap places with him. For the last thirty-four years of my life, I've spoken so many words; sometimes too many, even. I would give all the money in the world for you to be able to spend just one day of your life telling me what i should do. My heart is broken. It's beyond my imagination what you have to feel in moments like that. I can't picture it – you trying to break the wall to get to us, and no matter what, you can't.

Those thoughts in my head are like birds in the marketplace, trying to steal a piece of bread from my hand. I try to chase them away, but they keep on coming back. *"Why me? Why us? Why autism?"*

It could be worse, right?

I can't help looking at my friends' children – and i say this with affection – the smiley faces of smart kids. Maybe fate gave us a cheeky surprise because it was written somewhere that we could handle it? I guess we'll never find out.

I use the word 'fate' because for me, 'God' went out of use years before Maks was even born, although both of my children were baptized for their mothers' peace of mind. Don't get me wrong, I don't think of autism as a punishment, like many have suggested. I just smile and walk away, like when my mother in law said, *"you are just a waste of time and drive me crazy".*

We are human beings and we will handle whatever fate as in store for us. It doesn't mean we don't have good and bad days or weeks – sometimes we have to bend under the heavy burden of everyday troubles and issues. However, one step forward can put you back in the saddle. One good comment about a blog post or video I've made can give me a positive kick. I need to do that, and i need to share my thoughts, so everyone reading them can give me my wings. Give us wings!

DON'T BE AFRAID TO SAY 'NO' TO YOUR CHILD

Children with autism very often have issues with accepting the word *"no"*. Think about any child at the age of six – this magic word can make most kids go into scream-and-shout mode. Even adults have trouble understanding a simple *"no"*, *"now"*, *"tomorrow"*, or *"in a minute"*. Most often, autistic kids react because they don't have a sense of time. For people with ASD, hearing *"no"* can cause something like an earthquake without prior seismic activity. Kaboom! a child on the floor, crying and screaming. What now?

I'm going to tell you – nothing! Be consistent, even if it means strange looks from passers-by, implying that your child is not behaving, and suggesting you're a bad parent. I have moments like that almost on a weekly basis. I've learned to deal with them in a calm manner, and in extremely difficult or dangerous situations i just take my son in my arms and walk away with a sharp, *"No! Stop!"*. You need to understand that explaining something to our autistic son with long, full sentences, flooding him with streams of words is a little bit ridiculous. Short sentences mean understood sentences – or at least that's what I'm hoping for.

I remember when we had to stop using a pram due to Maks' age. Very often he didn't want to walk on his own and would ask me to carry him in my arms. Sometimes I'd give him a piggyback, but i never wanted to carry Maks around all the time, since it would teach him to demand it all the time, and because he needs physical activity. And let's face it, my body has its limits as well.

On one occasion, however, he didn't want to walk even 200-500 meters. We didn't have a car yet, and we'd been out for a genetic test. Maybe 100 meters from a bus stop, Maks sat down on the curb and refused to walk further. I tried to convince him to walk with me with no success. It was pretty busy around us, but i decided there was not much more i could do, so i joined him.

My eyes get wet when i think about it. a beautiful moment. People passing by, some giving us strange looks, and us cheerfully sitting there like that. Maks was looking up at the sky and me, smiling. Sometimes instead of a smile, a cry, but it was our time. Him and me – nothing else mattered. Someone stopped and asked if everything was ok, I looked up and beamed back at some random lady, answering, *"Yes, thank you. Everything is ok, my son is autistic."* The woman returned my smile with her eyes and gave us a wave. I felt like the best dad in the world. Maks got up from the curb and took my hand. We continued to walk. We might have been late ten minutes, but we were damn happy!

You realise how much you have in moments like that. You understand that some things are not such a problem, and you can get used to them. *"He's fine, he is just autistic"*, answered with a big smile on my face. Yes, for us it's just autism.

All i did was give my son the extra time he needed, yet we both learned very important lessons. Maks taught me patience and showed that sometimes stopping for a moment and waiting is priceless. I allowed him to experience having a father willing to let him process *"no"*, this word that can be so hard to accept.

Even as time passes, we still very often stop and take a seat on benches, curbs, and paths as people pass us by. Why not?

One thing to remember, my dear reader, is that the word *"no"* should never be used to express your expectations for any child, disabled or not. If you're trying to say, *"don't run"*, you should always add what you expect your child to do instead. Your child might not know whether you want them to slow down, take a seat, or lie on the floor. Give him or her a clue: *"please, instead of running away i want you to…"*. This is indeed a longer sentence, but it works much better. By choosing fully conscious interactions, you allow yourself to open up a little bit, while letting your child understand your expectations.

DON'T RAISE a DISABLED PERSON

From professional experience, I know for a fact that parents can get lost in the list of things which should or shouldn't be important when bringing up a child. Some of them would like their children to do exactly what they are told, a wrong approach. Another group of parents try to mirror their own dreams and unfulfilled plans in their kids, dragging them to every after-school club that might in their opinion be beneficial for the future. Don't forget, because of everyday hustle, sometimes we all turn into machines, doing things without thinking.

When i was studying early age education, one of my supervisors shared some very wise words with parents gathered at a meeting: *"If you really want to help us in educating and raising your children, teach them two things. The rest of the work should be left for us."* Those two things are essential enough that they can alter the plans of an entire day at nursery. Can you guess what i am referring to? You will be surprised: teach your kids how to put their shoes and jacket on.

Do you know how much time nursery nurses and assistants spend (or more accurately waste) staring at kids with sadness and confusion in their eyes, asking who will help them put their clothes on? Imagine 30 children in a classroom, all of them going outside at least twice a day. They always have to go through a process of dressing and undressing... You can see the point.

To be completely clear, it's not about them knowing how to tie shoelaces or do up a zip. It's only about putting on a jacket and knowing how to put shoes on and take them off. That's all. Simple! Later on, we can teach your child how to zip or tie or button up.

Those simple things are crucial. My own life has proved to me multiple times that when you're in a rush and your children are taking too much time to get ready, you end up stepping in. You help them with a jacket, scarf, hat, gloves, and shoes – it's better that than being late. Just as a matter of habit – chop-chop – clothes on, shoes on and we're on our way.

Maybe once in a while, it's good to give your child some extra time to find the right sleeve for their jacket, or which shoe is the left one. For a three-year-old, zipping up a jacket might be difficult, but that's a different problem. If we add time to everyday routines to show our children basic things, it will make them brave and independent human beings.

We have a bad tendency to do things in a hurry. I know that's the way the world is now. Unfortunately, if we skip what is necessary and do things robotically instead of letting our children learn, before we realise what's happened we end up with completely reliant seven and eight-year-olds; incapable of taking care of themselves or of doing things on their own – except maybe apart from the moment you give them an iPad...

It is possible to observe a generation of needy, dependent children growing up. a generation incapable of doing anything on their own, not to mention taking care of us, their parents, when we will need them. Not everyone has to agree with me on this, and not everyone does things automatically and in a rush. Nonetheless, three years of work in nurseries and primary schools allows me to be bold and state that we have a massive, growing number of children not able to perform basic, simple, everyday tasks.

You could say that this is what nurseries and schools are for – to teach. Yes, but not this stuff exactly. If educational institutions have to take over parental duties, there is no time left for the teaching the actual program! I won't even go into how it was when i was in primary school, when we were taught a lot of things way too early, with no consideration of individual needs and predispositions.

In Scotland, education is child-focused. The child is the centre of attention, not the teacher or the government. Thanks to that there is a balance. If a child is not so good in languages but clearly has good mathematical skills, nobody will force him or her to spend long hours trying to be amazing at both subjects. Teachers help them to achieve whatever is possible in the field they are best at.

Watch your children closely, teach them and praise them. Show them that being independent is its own best reward. That's exactly what i decided to do with my son, and I've watched him taking the first steps on his own with amazing happiness.

A MEDICAL CONDITION OR a SENTENCE?

I follow media campaigns in Poland closely, and i can see how different they are from those around Europe. Very often they highlight single words to make things simpler and get to people more easily. Don't get me wrong, I am glad that these campaigns exist, although in my opinion they need to be more accurate.

Autism is very often called an illness. What sort of illness? Is Down's syndrome an illness as well? Is cerebral palsy an illness? It's not such a big deal, but it makes me angry when people refer to it this way. You can get medication for illnesses.

Disability can appear at any stage of life – prenatal or after a child is born. People have wanted to argue with me about this so many times. That's why I'll highlight this again: **my son is not sick or ill**, and there is no medication that can cure him and change the way he is. What can help him is hard work and education, finding new ways of doing things, and adjusting so he can defeat obstacles. Not medication.

There is no point in going into how society in Poland treats mental disabilities. It's a taboo, a stigma. Those suffering from them are sentenced to exile. It's sad. I work with young people with different sorts of mental illnesses and what they go through every day is overwhelming. Add societal pressure and stigma from people around them, and they can often be pushed to marginalisation, self-harm and suicide.

Another phenomenon i come across very often is charities using slogans like *"Autism does not have to be a sentence!"* Really? What sentence are they talking about? No! Of course, autism is not a sentence. I contacted some of these charities, and what i heard is that it is easier to explain autism in these terms, and that it has a better effect on people. Let's be clear. The effect it had on me is pretty negative. The word "*sentence*" next to the words "*doesn't have to be*" sounds more like "*it is a sentence*". Charity slogans used to bring more attention to the subject of autism make my hair stand on end. I hope that one day I'll be able to change this approach somehow.

With this in mind, I joined a few discussion groups. From one of them, I even got a wristband with something similar to "*we're all crazy*" written on it. Unfortunately, thanks to an in-crowd mentality, members of this group were convinced that only they knew the absolute truth. I left the group very quickly and made sure that they were aware of the reason.

I would like to highlight that you can learn many interesting things meeting bloggers on discussion groups, although it's still far away from the ideal model. This is the main reason i don't take part in Polish discussion groups. I try as hard as possible to be a part of British autism charities and forums, and i now even work for one.

We have to teach society what disability really means, not only by slogans but through education. Starting from an early age, we should integrate with each other and talk about disability on a daily basis. It's not disabled people who need to adjust; it is for all of us to learn that we each have a full right to live our lives.

Don't forget though, this is only my opinion, and you can take it or leave it.

VACCINATION – EVIL OR NOT?

Many people blame autism on vaccinations, especially MMR (measles, mumps, and rubella). We decided not to go through with this vaccination prior to diagnosis, since there was negative publicity at the time about MMR and its connection with autism, and we feared the effect it might have.

Straight after Maks was diagnosed with autism, we decided to vaccinate him with MMR anyway – we didn't have much to lose. It didn't change anything, and things didn't get worse or better. Our daughter had the vaccination and we didn't notice any side effects.

People talk a lot about this topic, and you can find a lot of information about it on the internet. You can come to a conclusion on your own. I am not trying to convince anyone. It's your choice if you do it or not, and we all need to respect each other's opinion.

FRIENDS

We have a wide variety of friends, but in some ways it's hard to talk about them. When Maks was halfway through diagnosis, we moved from London to Edinburgh. We left most people behind but those we had just met in Edinburgh were a little bit scared and overwhelmed with Maks' disability. I think i was too idealistic or optimistic about the entire thing.

When people around me need someone or when something bad is happening in their lives, I am the first to help. I want to support them in confronting their troubles and issues. Yet some friends turned their backs on us. I came to appreciate why and forgave them. However, I don't need people around me who can't look me in the eye and say honestly: *"I don't want to be friends with you anymore"*. On the other hand, there are close friends who still don't know what to say and how to behave. Try to appreciate this and give them time like they did with you. For them, it's a new situation as well.

Most of us don't have a clue about autism: there's illness you can treat, and then there's the stereotype of the child sitting in the corner, swaying back and forwards with their eyes fixed on a single point. With time, anger and disappointment will be replaced with knowledge. You will learn the terminology, and after a few months of commitment you will become an expert.

WHO WILL YOU BECOME?

How far will you progress? Will you be independent?

One day we went for a hike with your grandmother. We spoke a lot about you, and i need to admit that i was shocked when she asked me with genuine curiosity, *"I wonder what Maks' wife and children will look like?"*

I have to tell you my son, that in this matter i wrote you off. I was focused so much on making sure you'll be as independent as possible that i completely forgot that one day you will have a great life. Maybe i was just being realistic but still, I don't have any right to write off a six year-old-boy. I felt mean. It's possibly because i know life and reality, but you're working so hard and you're progressing. Maybe i lack faith, or i maybe don't want to have false hope and disappoint myself. Forgive me. I am a jerk. Your father is a jerk. One more lesson learned.

It's all about how we handle our emotions. The issue lies in the fact that as parents we do a lot – we work, we bring you to classes and meetings, and we take an active part in your battle – but we always feel like we don't do enough. It's natural, but very damaging.

EMOTIONAL DEVELOPMENT

Recently i was wondering about how the development of our two amazing kids can be so different. What a massive responsibility as we have parents. Our decisions and emotions have a big impact on what sort of people our kids will be in the future. Looking at the process of Maks' development and how different it is from Livia's, I learned a lot about my children.

Until the moment Maks was diagnosed, I was assumed he would grow up in a normal way. Since children sometimes start to talk later, having a little human playing on his own was actually a great thing; other parents have kids constantly asking for attention. Now, years later, I know how mistaken i was...

Livia's birth changed everything, teaching me what being a parent really looks like. At the same time, I started college – early age education – and it was incredible how much i found out while studying. Education had a big impact on my approach to children, giving me patience, and understanding about behaviour and the importance of emotions. I had been fully convinced that Maks' outbursts were strictly connected with his autism. Obviously, this was partly the case, but i now know that in the early years of childhood, the brain is not efficient enough to deal with emotions, and most kids can't manage them very well.

When i look at Maks and Livia i can see some divergence in their affection and sensitivity. The older a child is, the better their control of emotions and feelings. He or she understands that some things are acceptable, that refusals and sadness are a part of life, and that with time can start to accept this.

Nonetheless, before the second year of life, every child can overreact to any new emotional stimulant and have outbursts, whether connected with happiness, sadness or anger. Toddlers are simply not capable of controlling emotions. Since the neural pathways in their brains allowing them to manage and understand emotions only start to be established after a few years, they don't have the appropriate tools.

In the case of autism, the assumption is that the neural pathways and networks responsible for emotions are built in a different way, or that they simply do not exist. It will be no surprise to state that autistic people don't handle emotions at all. I work with people whose emotional state switches between opposing poles multiple times a day. Maks can also be laughing uncontrollably one minute and burst into tears the next, and we could simply assume it's part of autism.

I'm sure the direct reason for such behaviours is not autism at all, but a lack of the tools necessary to deal with feelings, and the skills needed to process them on a daily basis. These are essential for the smooth transition from one mindset to another without the overwhelming feeling that the world is falling apart.

So that this can be understood this a little better, think about this question: how would you feel if you suddenly lost the ability to interpret emotions while watching TV? We're able to react to images we see, which is why we get sad or happy, and we laugh or get afraid. However, knowing something is just a movie means we are able to smoothly move on from one feeling to another. When a romantic comedy finishes we don't get sad, and after a horror movie the fear disappears because we can separate and turn off the connected emotions.

It doesn't work like that for a person with ASD; there's no off switch, and he or she can feel those emotions much longer, without understanding that it's just a part of a movie, or someone else's life. The same feelings can come back without reason at any time and get deeper and stronger because the autistic brain very often is not mature enough and does not develop. Maks can go into deep sadness or get euphoric, and our job as parents is to make sure we understand those behaviours and that we provide him with sufficient support.

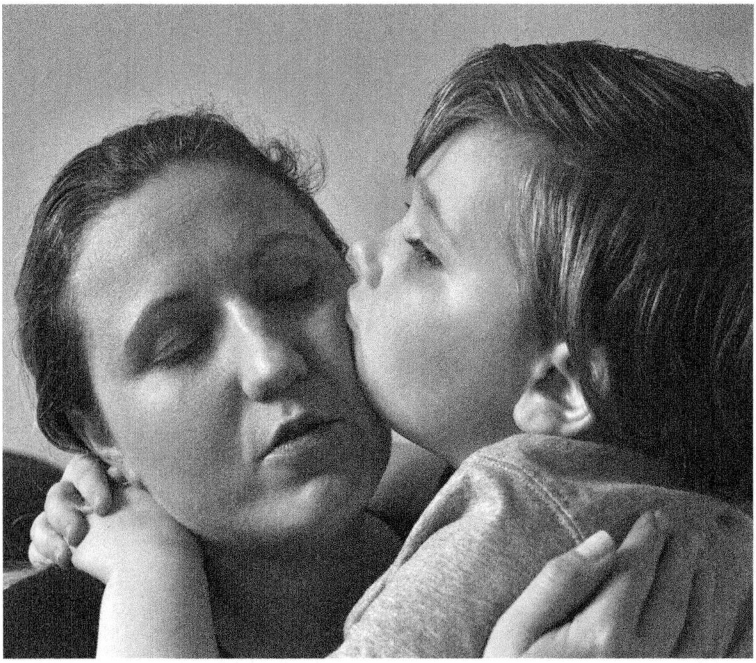

LEARNING YOU

We learn the whole of our lives. Most of all, we learn about each other; in relationships, at work. Also, we learn how to be parents. I was raised in a home where being smacked was normal; for something more serious, you might earn a whack with a belt or even a cable. As a rule, this was the type of upbringing kids had at that time. In the past it might have been a method of educating, but today giving your child a smack is something bad.

I always wanted to have my own family. My son was planned, the same as his sister. However, it was my daughter who allowed me to see how different the developmental stages of a typical child are from our autistic son. Nobody is born knowing what raising a child should look like or how to be a father, are they? People tell you that boys may start to speak later and walk later – in general, everything can happen later, and there's plenty of time for everything. This is true. Every child has a right time for everything, but dear reader, please remember to trust your own instincts.

***

I am learning about you every day, my son. Sometimes i lack patience, and there are moments when i just want to hug you and take on your autism for you. When you're screaming and throwing things around, I try to understand. When you're just being a naughty boy, I try to treat you just like a regular boy who is misbehaving, not like an autistic child. I've learned that we have to separate our children from autism. When things are obscured by the condition we should be more understanding, but we shouldn't look at our children through the lens of autism all the time. Doing this can cause more harm.

It's a fact – sometimes it's bigger than me. Sometimes i don't understand what you are trying to tell me or show me. It hurts. I fear those days when your mum and i have to guess or act from intuition. Like when you're ill or there's something bad happening. Very often it takes half the day to solve the mystery. Suddenly it becomes obvious that it's your tummy or you have a sore throat, and the sense of guilt never disappears. Damn… I should know better! Most important is to be aware that sometimes it can't be changed. Don't let remorse drive you crazy.

I am afraid of the day when there is something really serious going on, and i won't be able to decode the clues and guess what it's all about. Most of all, I fear the day when i am not going to be around. I promised myself that i would educate people about autism. I've been called a rock'n'roll autism dad. a long time ago, many things seemed so difficult, and i had troubles, issues. Well… today i know i just thought i had them. School of life, lesson number 12,388.

ME – a SENSITIVE PERSON

I wanted to avoid this chapter. I am fully conscious that sharing my past with readers will mean being unable to avoid comparisons and negativity. I came to the conclusion that in order to describe my fears and my feelings, and how i handled them, it's necessary to give a rough idea of my life. You can blow off some steam after this chapter.

I was born in a small town of about 13,000 people (and not much to do) in Pomeranian Voivodeship in the north of Poland. My home was in a typical Polish area of detached houses, on a street previously known as 1st of May Street, which became 3rd of May Street after the political system changed. My parents were amazing people, different to others and a mystery then and now, the same as their entire world. Deaf people raising kids with normal hearing – my older brother and me.

My father worked very hard and was pretty strict. He used physical force to motivate and discipline us. My mother was a lovely woman with a big heart who gave in much more easily. She allowed me whatever i wanted. Since the age of five, I was run ragged from post office to bank to council, translating between my parents and the rest of the world. My older brother was never interested in doing it. I was the one dragged away from activities – playing with other kids, video games, or lectures – as there was always something urgent to organise. That was my fate, my mission.

My brother was six years older. a good guy – a master of motivation through demotivation, a very well-known style, telling people *"forget about it – you'll quit anyway".* Although he always supported my love of music. He was the one who gave me money for my first guitar, cables, strings and amplifier. All of it earned by hard work in a car repair shop. Today he works for the police – criminal division. Respect! He even paid for part-time private school for me after i was kicked out of every single high school in my area. Thanks to him, I passed my GSCE.

It wasn't an easy childhood and we didn't have much, with dad investing all the money in refurbishing the house. Both our parents worked for an organisation helping disabled people, so i can say that disability was a normal thing in my childhood.

As a teenager i wanted to be a rock'n'roll guy. No change – it's still like that today. I formed my first rock band while still in high school. Two members, Marta and Lukasz, are still my best friends. Thanks, guys, for being with me! At the time, I was stunned by The Doors, Led Zeppelin, and the Polish band Dzem. After some time, I started to experiment with drugs and alcohol. Weed, speed, alcohol, pills, acid. One school, a second, and a third – there was no place for me anywhere. Nobody understood me – either at school or at home.

My 'play hard' stage came with Woodstock – a Polish punk rock music festival. That ended for me with rehab, in the mental institution in Lubliniec i mentioned previously. Later, I went back home and then ran away, hitchhiking to a Salesian convent in Trzciniec. Nobody knew; everyone thought i was at school. After this, I started school again in Czaplinek, but that ended fairly quickly as well. I was taken care of by a school friend's family. Extraordinary people. We're not in touch anymore. What a shame… Something went wrong, but i owe them a lot. My life.

Together with my family, I made the big decision that it was time for proper rehab. To be honest, this decision was taken out of my hands; I was just 17 years old. I was placed in rehab institution in Kamien Rymanski – a tiny village in north-west Poland. I was done after three months; I couldn't cope. I begged my parents to get me out of there. I wasn't even 18! Today, writing this book, I'm 34, and i can talk about it without any bigger problems. I pulled myself together. After i got out of rehab i met some good people, but again i was drawn to trouble. I left Poland at the age of twenty-three, and i went to the UK.

From the perspective of the past few years, I can say that the serious issues of a teenage boy are nothing compared with what life delivers us every day as the parents of disabled children. This is the reason why i wanted to share the story of my life. I want to show that i am not a silly boy, broken easily by little things. When you become a father and your child is suffering, when you feel helpless, you have every right to cry. Sometimes you have to. As one of my favourite philosophers Friedrich Nietzsche said, *"what doesn't kill you makes you stronger"*.

TAKE CARE OF YOUR MIND

Dear parent of an autistic child. On your own, you will fail. You and your partner. Talk to each other about your fears and doubts, about the things that hurt you. It's important. Don't let yourself store up pain, anger, and worries. Acknowledge your concerns and make some rules.

We live in the UK, immigrants in a new city for the last three years, in a pretty hermetic, closed world occupied by our family. Once or twice a year, we have a chance to go out together without the children. At the end of the day, it's hard to leave an autistic child alone with someone unfamiliar. We celebrate moments when we can relax, even if it's just a walk or going out for dinner somewhere. If you have an opportunity to use grandparents or any other family members or friends, do it and go out on regular basis. You need to keep yourself sane.

Take a break, even from each other. My wife and i send each other out for a coffee or a drink with friends. We also have a rule that at least once a year we each go away on our own. My wife usually goes to Poland or to see old friends from London. I am similar – I organise 'lads' trips' with my best friend from London – beer, spa, fishing, Poland, Scandinavia. Take turns caring for your autistic child. Take care of yourself and take care of your emotional state.

***

Very often, I talk to my wife about things that are bothering me – if i am feeling down, or nervous and anxious. I don't want her to find out about it when it's too late, or when she will suddenly become a victim of my moods. I tell her that i am all over the place, and she either knows how to explain it and sort it out or sends me to the gym or for pint with friends.

I do the same for her. For women it's even more difficult, after carrying a child for nine months under their hearts. Try anyway. Send her shopping, keep on repeating that you love her, and that she is the most beautiful woman you have ever seen. Let her feel it.

Sometimes my wife and i feel like we're the only people we can depend on. The four of us are like a cosy little planet, with nobody asking us any questions. We're like the Little Prince and the Rose. In springtime, we wake up and go out into the outside world. Everything has its own rhythm; there's always an order in craziness.

WHAT WILL YOU SAY?

I am a support worker. I work mostly with adult autistic people, helping them in everyday life, by promoting their choices and their independence. When working with clients suffering from autism or other disabilities, it is very important for me to understand their relationships with other people.

Some of my clients – children, teenagers or even adults – are often aggressive, or don't behave in the most nice or pleasant way. I agree that this not easy to accept, but most important is realising that none of this behaviour is on purpose, and that it shouldn't be taken personally. Many of the things happening in their lives springs from autism. They can be explained as reactions to a particular environment or stimulus. Frustrations or tensions are connected to the autistic brain translating factors in one way or another, or simply not being able to handle them.

I know that today's world is focused on political correctness, rules, and tolerance. However, the autistic world is not set according to regular social rules, and there are no political barriers. Personally, I think we need to expect more understanding for disable people than from ourselves.

Try putting yourself in the shoes of a disabled or mentally ill person sometime. It is extremely easy to create slogans and label people. We feel comfortable when judging others, writing anonymous comments under articles on the internet. Hate is something that disabled people experience every day. Mocking and laughing about disabilities and other abnormalities is a common thing. Trust me, I know what i am talking about. As a child and teenager, I came across stupid comments about my deaf parents so many times. Yet, my weapon was calmness and down-to-earth explanation of what their disability was all about.

Now i often joke about my son – sometimes i say his autism is just a decoy, and that Maks is undercover, secretly planning to conquer the world. Remember – joking is for people and hate is for cowards.

CHANGES INSIDE OF ME

I am starting to look at the world differently. Friends, relationships, my problems and other people's issues look different. There are moments when i have to stop for a second and think about what all those people are talking about. Sometimes, my inner voice shouts, *"what the f**k?!?!"* with respect to people around me, and i have the feeling that some of their problems aren't real. When you're facing diagnosis, disability, illness, the death of a someone close, or some other traumatic event in your life, everything changes.

Sometimes i switch to my 'neutral' gear: I am able to chill out, stand on the side and rethink everything, even in the middle of the day. I can retreat from the rat race, look at the situation from a different perspective and reach a conclusion, able in the end to smile to myself and say that everything is just fine. Then i can jump back on to the right track and run towards making my dreams come true. Positive thinking is extremely important.

I refuse to watch the news on TV or listen to radio news stations simply because they affect me in a negative way. I might lack the most recent knowledge about the political situation around the world and in other fields, but i can't handle the huge amount of sorrow and negativity found in the press. I think this is healthy, at least in my case. The disability of a child brings a lot of heartache. I want to limit bad feelings, so i can focus on the positive things in my life. That's the way i am. You should be yourself, my dear reader, and always remember that disability in your life will always change something. Give yourself time for reflection and give yourself time for tears. Don't be afraid of making decisions based on your feelings and your current state of mind.

In my case, for example, after taking the pros and cons under consideration, I decided to work only 30 hours a week. Luckily, I can afford to do this, and the result is that i can spend more time with the kids and focus on my education. I can move towards a better understanding of autism and help other parents and their children. My work – what you're reading – is the proof. I have time, and i have spent the last three years on self-development. In the future, I would like to become an expert in the autism field.

FEELINGS

There are a few moments in my life i look back on in a different way after my son's diagnosis. Knowing what i know now, in those situations i would most likely change things i said, or just shut up.

Before Maks' was officially diagnosed in the UK, I approached many charities helping parents and children touched by autism. Many times, I was shown the door after being told there wasn't much they could do without this single piece of paper from the NHS. I felt like the dregs of society, and it hurt badly, but now i understand it. Sometimes when i go back to my blog posts from that time, I can see how much pain and sorrow was pouring out of me. Yes, those were my feelings. Today i understand that i wasn't being treated differently from anyone else, and that those organisations had their reasons, since their work is based on funding, and they have to report the number of diagnosed children in order to receive money.

Furthermore, now i know that there are charities in a position to help people before diagnosis, or even before they receive a GP's referral. I am happy about this, as it means people are able to get help much earlier than before. Parents don't have to feel the way i did three years ago, when the world fell apart and i felt that all the doors were closed to me. In those situations, your sorrow is overwhelming, and you feel unwanted.

At this point, if you are friends of any family with an autistic child, just be there for them. We don't expect anything else from you. Just be. Don't talk about your issues – believe me, we have already enough of our own, and don't try to comfort us. Don't escalate our anger by asking, *"how could they do that to you?!"* Just be. Make a cup of tea, sit down beside us, and be.

THE PARABOLA OF LIFE

I've wondered for a long time how i find it possible to do so many things at the same time, and why i add extra duties and set new goals whenever anything is ticked off my 'to do' list.

My source of energy is my family. Sometimes, when i slow down a little bit, I turn around and look at Maks and Livia. My kids are most important – their development defines who they will be in the future, while my development defines what sort of father i will be for them. In autism, there are times for growth and times when everything slows down and shrinks. Sometimes progress is visible every day, but there are also days when things our child could easily do are not achievable anymore. And when our frustration levels are sky-high, because everything was going so well!

Take a deep breath and don't get upset. Our kids are mavericks. Sometimes they find the solution on their own, and very often it's one which wouldn't occur to neuro-typical people like us. Every autistic person is programmed differently and looks for independence in their own way. My son found a way to express his thoughts and feelings by using quotes from cartoon movies. Would you come up with an idea of this sort? Most likely not. So, don't expect that an autistic person will think like we do. Give him or her time to discover their own solution and ask if help is needed – but do not impose, and never force them to do anything.

Children with ASD understand the word *"no"* in a better way than others. It's the first word about their existence they are sure of, and they know how to use it with extraordinary firmness.

Emotions, development and massive frustration, bonded to an inability to understand others – and most of all themselves – is a lot to deal with. Wait for the signs. When asked if he needs anything, Maks gets very nervous and repeats: *"I do not agree with it!"*, a quote learned from one of his cartoons. I know after hearing these words that i need to give him a choice, or drop the subject, otherwise he will get stressed with the huge amount of unwanted, random words pushing straight into his head.

Give it some thought. Ask your autistic child to show you. Limit your words to short sentences. Time, time, and time again. Always think about the fact that people with ASD see the world and think in a different way – we need to give them time to process information. It's a real lesson in patience. Also consider that with autism, everything moves in cycles. Always. Just like in life: there is time for progress, a time for harvesting, a time for rest, and a time for preparing the field for the next cycle.

HAVING HOPE

Remember, that progress and regression are always chasing each other. Your child can take some steps forwards and move backwards straight after. It's difficult to accept but natural, so always keep it in mind. Sometimes progress comes in phases: your child develops quickly, learns new words and gains new skills but then stops for some time. Follow him or her in their own rhythm. Be patient and give yourself time. Even when there's regression, don't worry. Look for solutions. It's important that the situation is constantly changing. Share your thoughts and emotions.

For example, I've joined a monthly group called Dad's Night. Fathers of autistic children, meeting together in the pub to for a beer – joking, laughing and chatting about life. Each of us does something different for a living – there's an IT guy, someone else working in sales, and one guy working from home. We have a man who does calculations for Formula 1, and another with a Ph.D. in chemistry, who is main carer for his kids. It's great that in relation to autism, we understand each other without using any words. Our children are different ages and on different parts of the spectrum, but what really matters is that we are united in one thing, even if we're different in everything else. It's the perfect opportunity to build amazing understanding.

Meeting once a month is enough to recharge your batteries with positive energy, feel the power of unity, and get a good hangover.

Look for other people and remember: have hope and give hope. You're never alone. You can even place an advertisement on the internet saying that you're looking for other parents – there will be definitely be people who will reply and meet with you.

FIGHT

I don't want you to think that my world is different than yours. True, I have been in the UK for eleven years, I have a family and we're doing OK. However, we went through a lot separately and together. I know that diagnosis sometimes destroys relationships which are already falling apart when both of you are feeling overwhelmed. The best part is that it's nothing unusual.

The world sometimes spins unrealistic stories about heroic people who don't yield under any pressure or weight. The reality is completely opposite. Most of us have cracked and broken bones from fighting everyday problems. It is important to understand that every child – healthy or not, planned or unplanned – needs properly developed, healthy relationships. a child can sense how its mother reacts to his or her emotions. If she is constantly stressed, how can a child be able to develop in the correct way emotionally?

Dear parents! If you decide to separate, at least fight for a healthy relationship with each other, for your kids. I write about this from experience – some time ago i wasn't able to understand it. Maybe one day it will be forgiven...

Talk about your child and how you want to raise them. Don't haggle, and don't say that one of you loves your child more than the other. Try to explain to your child what is happening. I know it's sometimes difficult, but don't get your kids involved in the battles you might be having with each other; don't say this is OK.

It requires great acting skills, but don't speak about your ex-partner in anything other than a good and pleasant way.

Even if positive words are very hard to come by. It's not about saying that this person is great and loving, if in reality they are an abusive alcoholic. Sometimes it's better not to say anything at all than to say to your child, *"your father is drunk again and is being abusive".*

If your child asks you why their other parent is acting in a particular way, answer that she or he has a problem to deal with. Look for solutions which don't involve emotional interference with the image of a parent. a child sees a lot and understands pretty well what's happening, so talking about a second parent in a bad way is just sad.

With a disabled child everything is much more difficult, especially when they are without linguistic skills and the ability to communicate and make connections. What can be done? Be together when going for any appointments, swap with each other when taking care of your child, and let each other rest. If you're convinced that the only solution is to separate, have the balls to live with it and don't blame anyone else for making the choice.

DEPRESSION

A silent, awkward and – you could easily say – a bashful illness. There is nothing more deceptive, and we struggle with it every day in our home. My wife is a brave fighter. It's a difficult subject for many, including her. She cancelled visits to her psychologist many times because she felt awkward and ashamed. For me, it's a hidden and very sensitive problem. I know there is no way that depression is a sign of weakness.

Sometimes i notice that you're lacking strength, that you feel everything is bigger than you and i know you're crying when I'm not home. Sometimes i close myself in the bathroom and i hide my face in my hands, crying like a child.
I can see that you have mood swings, that you feel like taking your last breath. I know that it's so hard for you and I'm sad because of it, but I'm by your side. I'm thinking about you. I know that you have migraines, moments of tiredness and you feel alone and weak. Remember, it's not true.
You're the strongest woman i have ever known. Each of us been through a lot. We will face more problems, and nothing will break us. It's hard for both of us, sometimes we stumble, but what matters is that we get up and go forward.
Our children have our support, they feel safe and receive all love they need. It's not a sign of weakness, but being great, being strong, but most of all being HUMAN.

Remember!
Your Loving Husband

I support my wife, I worry about her, and i am by her side. I try to understand her, and i know that it can be very shameful for her. Sometimes you can be under the impression that when something happens, it touches every aspect of your life. I will not lie, it's hard for all of us. For me as well. Our son's disability has had a massive impact on our mental health. My wife is bravely dealing with her troubles, and I'm trying to help her in any way i can. I can see sometimes that her glow is disappearing, and that she's running on fumes. In those moments i need to try even harder.

There's nothing shameful in depression. It's another strong stereotype, another myth which can be demolished if we find some time to read more, talk about it and open our minds. I know very well how hard it can be for my wife. Most of the time, I'm working or studying. She has to take care of our home and two children. Of course, I try to give her hand with everything and take some of the pressure off her, but it's her who spends more time with Maks and Livia. Our son's autism and the development of our daughter has a bigger impact on her than me. I sometimes blame myself, because I'm busy all the time – my way of dealing with it takes on a completely different character. Nevertheless, she can always depend on me. I will always be there for her.

I know the fact that we're far away from her family and that we don't have many friends over here has big significance for her. Ewa has a right to feel lonely and alone. Depression is hard, but it will not stop us. There will be a lot of bad and good days, but we will not give up.

IT LIFTS ME UP

I have tears in my eyes, son.

I'll go into why in a second. Maybe for you, my dear reader, it will be something you will struggle to understand rationally. Or it could be the opposite, and it will seem so normal you will start to wonder why you are reading this book.

It's the 3rd of November. a day like any other, full of challenges, work, and screaming kids – *"I want this, I want that"*, or to be more specific, *"I don't want this, I don't want that!"*. You – Maks – are falling asleep on the living room sofa after a shower, covering your head with two pillows exactly the way you like, and starting to drift away. At nine in the evening i take you in my arms to move you to bed. Doesn't sound like a big deal – nothing, right? While moving you from the sofa, you say one word – and i hear it very clearly – ***"Daaaad"***.

You said *"Dad"!* For the first time, it wasn't echolalia: a random word repeated after me or someone else. You were six years, two months and two days old on the day when you said *"Dad"* for the first time on your own. DAD!

Yes, my son – I'm here and i will be waiting for more to come. It was worth waiting for, and for you my son, I can wait forever. That word made everything else disappear, changing the way you look at everything around you. My son, at the age of six, said *"Dad"!* I was over the moon! Seriously, my brain was bouncing with happiness, I couldn't fall asleep, lying in bed and smiling to myself like mad.

Even if i have to wait another 30 years for the next *"Dad"*, even if it never happens again, I would like you to know that those are the moments i live for. For us, those moments are light in the land of shadows, brightening the darkness of reality. You, my dear reader, have your own special moments for sure. I'm joining you in your happiness. Goodnight!

ARE YOU DOING YOUR BEST?

I remember a video shared by a well-known Polish coach from one of his events. He brought up a very important subject: *"Am i doing what I'm doing to the best of my abilities?"* Every time i watch it, it brings tears to my eyes. However, I'll give you the answer: no, I don't do my maximum. And you don't especially do so either. Now, you're going to say this is nonsense.

I signed up for college, I changed my job, and i became aware of self-development and what i wanted our life to look like. I thought that if Maks can fight and do his best every day, what sort of a man does it make me if i spend my time messing around? I needed to move forward. You could say that this is normal and part of the obligation of having a family, but that's not the point. The point is to do your best and even more every day, focusing not only on yourself but devoting yourself to others.

Stop moaning, do something with your life, change something, move forward! The Polish personal development guru Michal Wawrzyniak (aka Kolcz Majk) talks about the everyday fight of parents of disabled children – strong and beautiful words. *No excuses!* Today, after all this time, when people start to complain i just smile; I'm happy with all i have. I'm glad I've learned how to not complain.

Everyone is unique, so i don't want to generalize. In our case, our 'tragedy' brought us closer and made our family stronger. It gave our life bigger purpose. I have a dream for the future – adoption. Most likely, I would like to adopt a disabled child. Would you be brave enough? I hope that answer is yes!

Don't create fake problems, and don't live your life just for the sake of it. Do your best every day. Some time ago i saw an article about the British cycling team. Someone decided to improve each aspect of the team by 1%, – everything connected with practice and training, from start to finish. From the bike frames, through to the screws in each bike. They tracked the route of every team member to training, including the coach himself. They checked the sleeping patterns of the crew, and they improved the shape of pillows. They even improved the way team washed their hands to decrease the possibility of catching a cold or the flu.

If you use this sort of plan in parts of your life, you will notice the real beauty of routine. You'll see how much can change and how far you can get. Smile more often. Control bad emotions. Love what you've been given and push as hard as possible.

We push for Maks...

STOP

Can you stop for a minute? Make yourself a hot drink – tea or coffee – open a can of beer or anything else you like and sit down. Find a moment just for yourself. Switch off your phone or your TV, go for a drive to somewhere where there is just you and nobody else. Stop. Look in front of you and be. For a man tilting at windmills every day, it is worth living a moment of reflection and cogitation.

I'm not telling you to switch off, but to find a moment for thought and reflection about whether you really have to chase and run so much. Don't think about work, but about the fact that parents of disabled children usually have to do exactly the same amount of work as everyone else, plus hundreds of other things related to their kids' lives.

Sometimes you're allowed to give things a miss, for example, going to see your in-laws. Stay at home, listen to music and think about what you could do differently. How can you save precious energy?

Very often we're under the impression that we have to do many things at the same time. Yes, we do – but we can do things smarter and better, benefitting everyone around us. Remember that you can burn out, at work, as well in your relationship. If you push too hard, there can be a moment in which you will fall down. Who will be there to help you get up?

Remember, you have to take good care of your physical and emotional health. Your children need you operational, not having to take a breather after walking 100 meters. They need you cheerful and optimistic, not constantly pissed off and irritated with everything happening around you.

Make conscious choices. Maybe sometimes it's worth going part time and changing your hours so that you work less. Remember, your family is most important, so talk about it with your boss and co-workers. Each and every one of them can learn something, and thanks to you they will be aware of the issues parents of disabled children have to face every day. Some of them might be stubborn and won't believe it, but because you tried, your conscience will be clear.

Be an ambassador for your child, with pride rippling your chest. Our children confront everything with a brave face, and you have to be with them. You can't even imagine how proud i am of the fact that my son is autistic. He is mine and i love him and his burden, and not someone else.

PRECIOUS FAMILY MOMENTS

We have a pretty big family. My wife has four brothers, each of whom has a wife and child, and i have a brother with two kids. There's also my mum and my amazing mother-in-law. We don't visit our family in Poland very often. Once or twice a year, we try to go there for three or four weeks. It's beautiful that our connection is pretty good, even though they see Maks and Livia so rarely. My kids have amazing uncles and aunties, and their grandmothers are the best, like grandparents usually are.

I don't about autism talk at all with most of them. There's too many differences between us. I don't feel a need to externalize my feelings, but i have massive respect for them because they ask questions, they're there for us, and every time we visit they do their best to spend time with my kids. Sometimes they take the kids for a full day. Silence… and emptiness. My wife and i can go with for a walk to town together, holding hands. Usually one of us needs to hold Maks' hand while the other pushes a pram.

Although i appreciate their happiness, I am envious of people with grandparents, uncles, and aunties close by – someone that's happy to look after the kids for a few hours or over the weekend. We emigrated on our own so we're not so lucky. It's one of the downsides of living abroad far away from home. Please, appreciate what you have.

Parents of disabled children like us sometimes refuse to take help given by others. At the end of the day, we are the ones who knows our kids best. It's often more reassuring when we can see that everything is OK with at least the corner of an eye;

that way we can read every little change of facial expression before an outburst starts.

Last October my mother-in-law visited us. What an amazing woman! She has been through a lot (seriously, enough to write another book), and also has a disability, raising five kids with only one fully functioning hand. She stayed with our kids and we went out for dinner and cocktails. We're able to find the opportunity to do something like that maybe once a year. Can you imagine? We leave home without the kids once a year, yet every time i instantly miss them, and think about them constantly. Maybe if we had more chances to go out alone, we could get used to that. Now? The dog let off the lead still comes perfectly to heel.

If you have a chance to do so, plan nights out with your spouse, as often as possible. Go on! Just remember to keep your phone switched on.

***

It makes me smile that our family accepts Maks the way he is. Although sometimes they ask things like, *"did you try feeding him with this, or that?"*. My wife and i just smile at each other and try to gently educate them.

My brother was afraid of Maks; he didn't know how he should approach him. In the end, he gave it a shot, coming closer and saying, *"hey, Maks"*. Maks obviously even didn't notice his presence. He didn't try again – not everyone is born to cross the boundaries. You'd hope the way we educate the next generation will make this sort of issue a thing of the past, right?

I know that some have a more difficult journey with the people closest to them. I've heard from friends about their families blaming overprotection, sugar, bad diet, bad teachers or even us – the parents – for autism. Trust me, statements like, *in the old days, kids ate everything and didn't shower every day and were completely healthy,"* do not help at all. Neither does mention of the theory that there were no disabled children in the past. They did exist, but they were closed up in medical institutions or put in sheds, unfortunately. We're in a different age now, and diagnosis is at a more advanced level.

PITY IS BAD

I think about the fate of our family, how people react to our children, and about how their lives will turn out. I don't want any pity, and i don't want to hear any fretting about Maks being such a poor boy and us being an unlucky family. Maks, like every other child, needs love, affection, attention, and contact with others, as well as education to lead him through life. Our approach to Maks – by the way, the same as with every other kid – needs to stay 'child-centred', focused his needs as a child. For example, those needs related to education have to be fulfilled in a way that he will be given the best chance to have an independent life and development.

My dear reader, if the only thing you have for us is pity, it means you have given up on us. If all you can give us is mercy, you're assuming we're losers, and we've already failed. We don't feel like that – we feel the complete opposite, and we're not limited by negative stereotypes of families with an autistic child. We're fighting every day, and there's no chance we will stop. You can watch us closely and cheer us on, but don't dare let us hear you sighing. You can support us, be a fan or an enemy, ignore our voice or pretend you don't notice our presence, but never give up on us.

Looking at the world from their own perspective, disabled children don't feel these sorts of emotions. It never crossed the minds of my deaf parents to think they were lost causes or second-class citizens just because they couldn't hear. They had lives and they made progress. My father built our family home with his own hands, and my mum took care of a household and raised kids. They said, "*the sky is the limit*". Disability creates new paths; pity creates barriers.

Talk to people, ask questions and use your brain. Nowadays independent thinking is a gift. I love answering questions and talking about autism. After every conversation i have, in my mind it means that another person is more aware of what autism as a disability is.

There are no awkward questions. Parents of disabled children prefer answering difficult questions and educating society than fighting ignorance, lying, and harmful, unfair stereotypes. They say that fear makes things look twice as bad as they are. It's because of fear, vague statements and insufficient knowledge about a subject that stereotypes are created in the first place. That's my opinion – a little bit harsh and very pragmatic. You might not agree with it, but as long as you keep your opinions to yourself, I respect them.

SILENCE PAYS OFF

This short chapter offers a light-hearted look at ways of avoiding getting a punch in a face or otherwise putting your life at risk while around an autistic parent. With this in mind, I decided to create a short list of things you shouldn't say during a conversation with parents or carers of an autistic child. Not least when their hearts are bleeding and they don't know where to start in their battle with the condition.

I beg you to not say, *"maybe he'll grow out of it".* This doesn't help at all. Waiting for a child to grow out of it decreases the chance of early diagnosis and effective therapy that can work. It's better to say, *"I know you're worried, so maybe it would be a good idea to consult a specialist to see what they think about it".*

The next one on the blacklist is, *"oh, he doesn't look autistic".* Don't compare any child with an autistic child. Avoid saying *"my friend's son was autistic as well, and at the same age he could go out and stay at home on his own".* If you want to stay alive don't compare a child with ASD with any other kid, theoretically healthy or not.

The next forbidden piece of 'good advice' is saying something like: *"just tell him to do this/eat that/wear this/say that…."* No – unfortunately, that's not the way it works. Those things are simply not doable. There's no such power in this world.

One day i heard this from an old lady (and it's a miracle i didn't hurt her): *"a few smacks, and he will know how to behave".* If you value your life, better stay silent. Seriously, the cause of autism is not bad behaviour or spoiling a child.

Also prohibited are suggestions such as, *"are you giving him holy water/vitamins/fruit/broccoli?"* No! Mud baths, prayers or exorcism are not taken into consideration either. After saying, *"it's God punishment,"* you can expect to turn up on the missing persons list (joke!).

All sentences from more senior people starting with *"in the old days..."* or, *"when i was young..."* can be answered with a simple smile. It's only out of respect for age that we meet such lack of knowledge by hiding our fists in our pockets and gently biting our tongues, finishing each conversation with a cheerful smile. Blaming vaccinations or Chernobyl and offering prayers will also not have any effect on me.

You're banned from giving a diagnosis if you're not a medical graduate, even if a child shows all possible symptoms of ASD. Parents should hear it from a professional, so even if you're a hundred percent sure, shut your mouth. The best you can do is help arrange a doctor's visit. I have seen many potentially autistic kids, but before diagnosis has been made, I don't have any right to suggest anything, even though i work with autistic people, I am an educator, and my son has ASD. No. It's not the right thing to do.

I also need to add that asking the father or mother of an autistic child whether their son or daughter has any superhuman powers is simply out of order. Not every single autistic person is Rain Man; the majority of them can barely cope with everyday reality. Don't compare different cases of autism with each other, and certainly don't do it with neuro-typical and autistic children. Remember also that Asperger syndrome is a form of autism.

THE NEXT STAGES OF COMMUNICATION

I would like to make you sensitive of the fact that communication with a disabled child is an individual matter. It's also an area in which development can progress in many different ways, even when the steps look pretty much the same in most cases. We worried and wondered what we could do to make Maks' life less frustrating – something that would make his communication with us and the outside world easier.

Despite the all good things given by Scotland and the specialist healthcare available, I think there were mistakes made to begin with. Institutions providing help with communication between children and their parents should focus on the basics first rather than setting targets too high. At the age of four, Maks got his first iPad, with a special app on it helping him to interact with people around him. Of course, I can admit that it gave us and our son an amazing variety of possibilities, but with time we realised that we needed to work on developing basic communication skills.

The iPad app, Proloquo2Go, has some fantastic options. It's an electronic version of the picture exchange communication system (PECS) with an included voice simulator. The application offers many creative choices and is highly flexible. Unfortunately, with this hyper-optimistic approach, we didn't pay enough attention to the fact that Maks should have been shown how to connect to us with basic skills first. Our son mostly played with the program, listening to words and repeating them, but he wasn't communicating with us.

I'd like to highlight that you should never choose to cut corners while working with autistic children – you need to go through each stage, one by one. We decided to go back to the beginning. Luckily, Maks started to go to school and he was able to learn the essential skills needed.

At this point, it is worth understanding an outline of how communication is built in the case of pre-school aged children. The best way is to start from the simplest elements using indication techniques, where you might display an object together with associated actions.

For example, if we want to demonstrate changing a nappy, we would hold the nappy, and calmly show it to the child. We would then take him or her with us to the place where the nappy is to be changed, continually using words strictly connected with the activity. With time, the child will react in the desired way. When we produce a nappy, he or she will know what is going to happen next. Obviously, it goes without saying that different activities prompt different emotions.

When a child masters this first level, you can raise the stakes by replacing the object itself with a picture of it. Photos or pictures of a particular item can help us move to the next stage. This way we can teach flexibility, with time and the development of language also becoming important steps towards free communication. As a child comes to understand that a picture also means an associated activity, it creates a link. It's no longer that we're just waving a laminated picture in front of them, but instead that the item on the picture indicates a relationship to a certain word, and a particular expected behaviour. They will understand that we expect them to follow us. There is even a chance that they will use the repeated word.

The last step involves an individual, personalised expression of needs. In this phase of learning communication skills, our child should be able to show us a particular picture, and by doing so convey to us that they want something to drink or that their nappy needs changed.

Only after this can we then start thinking about developing full communication through PECS, together (if possible) with speech. a child should start by building simple, short questions and requests. When this is mastered, we can finally go on to use electronic devices and applications like those mentioned above.

As you can see, we would have missed a lot if we hadn't decided to go back to the beginning and start working with Maks from scratch. Today, Maks is able to come to us or his teacher with two pictures in the right order, and either stick them to a board or hand them over – amazingly even using the words he needs sometimes. This way of communicating is still not fully developed, but for example, he can get his iPad and his pictures, come to us and say, *"I want iPad"*, using fingers and voice to correctly point out specific illustrations for the request.

I believe that with time we will be able to use more words, with Maks' school consistently increasing the choice of elements available on his communication board. We have *"I want"*, *"I see"* and around 20 nouns. As parents, every new word is an occasion to celebrate and be happy. Try to appreciate the work of teachers and therapists, even in small successes. Be patient and remember the necessity of every step.

Some time ago i was participating in a seminar about communication for parents of children with ASD. At the end of it, participants were told to write a letter to themselves, listing one goal they would like to achieve with their children. My stated ambition was for Maks to stop relying on nappies and be able to use the toilet on his own. I completely forgot about it. Exactly a year after the workshop, I received a small parcel. Inside was the piece of paper with my oh-so-distant dream for Maks written on it. That day, I realised that it had been six months since Maks had come out of nappies and started using the toilet on his own! Some highly autistic children never become capable of doing this, and when i wrote it down, it seemed almost impossible. It's a beautiful example of how much can be achieved and how wrong i was! Maks – Dad is very proud of you!

F**K

It's not always so beautiful. I'm reminded of a situation from about a year and a half ago. Maks was in nursery. We live in an area where you can meet a lot of our fellow countrymen from different backgrounds, like in any big city. One day Maks came back home and was just about to start eating his dinner when he stepped on a toy. Suddenly he said, *"oh fuck!"* I looked at my wife, and she gave me a look back.

"Did i hear what i think i heard?", I asked Ewa.

"I'm not entirely sure...", she answered.

Minutes later, everything was back to normal, with Maks playing while we continued our previous conversation. a bucolic scene. Again, out of nowhere after stumbling or something we heard him say, *"oh fuck!"* Complete shock! It subsequently happened numerous times. Consternation. Maks started swearing several times a day in different situations, like when something happened suddenly, or when he got scared. Mostly in the kind of moments this sort of language might come out of an adult's mouth.

I should add that it was a period when Maks was non-verbal and didn't talk at all. *"Great,"* I thought, *"a non-verbal son, and when he starts talking, his first words are swearing!"* It seemed funny, but scary at the same time. I mentioned it to a teacher at school and we had a chat about it, finding out that one of the boys in Maks' nursery group used some pretty coarse language. I listened in on him, and i had to admit that even i didn't have such a rich vocabulary – straight from the rough end of town. We didn't draw much attention to Maks' swearing in the beginning, hoping that it would go away by itself.

However, after over a week of it, we needed to explain. Luckily, he eventually stopped.

No matter what state we're in and which language we use, how comical is it that our brains learn swearwords first?

SCHOOL OF LIFE

I often wonder if there's anything left to surprise us. I've worked with autistic people for many years, and I've encountered every possible difficulty. I've always said that we have to try to understand where particular behaviours come from and what triggers them. Sometimes these are outside factors, but there are cases where it is the autism itself.

Recently I've noticed that Maks sometimes becomes aggressive. After i refuse to give him a certain thing, or his mum doesn't let him do something else, he starts to punch us. Until lately, he had never raised a hand. Eventually, we linked it to something he had become a victim of quite recently. For about two weeks, he had been coming back from school with scratches. We intervened.

Obviously, I understand that children starting school can be as scared and petrified as our son. They can be afraid, they can be anxious, and most of the time children in these situations can become aggressive, pushing and scratching others. Then, attack becomes the best protection.

After having a chat with the teacher our guesses were confirmed. Our Maks was always one of the peaceful children, but some of the new students in the group were aggressive. Maks was beaten and pushed around until he learned how to say *"no"* – by which time he'd also learned how to push and beat others...

What is important is to teach your child that this is not the right way to behave and then explain how to settle things in a different way. I know that more challenges will come. When Maks reaches adolescence, his hormones will start cocking a snook at us and himself. It's all ahead of us, but whatever happens, we are stronger together. We will always love and support each other.

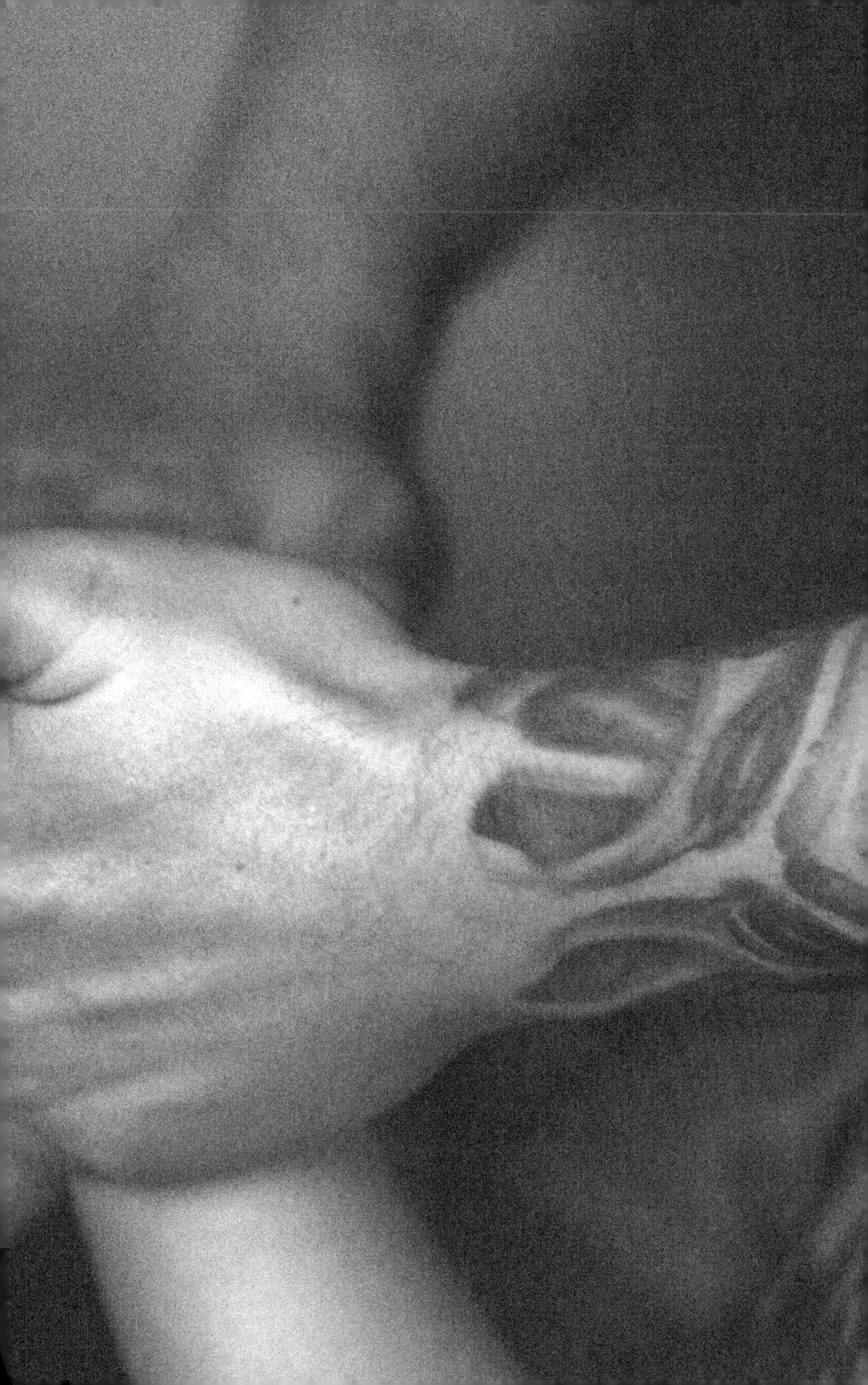

BEAUTIFUL MOMENTS

Our children give us many beautiful moments, and the beginning of every stage in their lives is a new milestone for us. It's no different when talking about autistic children. Their development can take more time, and important moments sometimes come as a surprise – almost always bringing an emotional load.

Maks – if this book were able to grow with you my son, there would be the chance to describe many of these occasions. However, I would never finish writing it. Luckily, I have my own blog, so i can record events and my reflections online. Here is just one of these heart-melting stories.

Once, because of a mix-up, I had to go to work on a Thursday evening. Your mum had a Spanish class, so we had to ask our neighbour, a friend, to take care of you and your sister for a couple of hours while we were both out. Livia fell asleep surprisingly early and you, my dear son, gave us some unforgettable memories.

When your mum left the house and i was at work, you came to the door, and with tears in your eyes, shouted, *"Mum! Daddy! Baby!"* Most of the time you were unconcerned when we left you, or when the two of you were alone with someone else. Our neighbour called your mum. Put on speaker, she told you that the baby was sleeping in the room next door and that mum and dad would be back soon.

Dear reader, you're probably thinking, *"what's so extraordinary about this? All children miss their parents!"* Well, it is extraordinary and unusual, because at this particular moment our son reached the threshold of a new stage of his mental development. Maks' emotional development had started to interlock with his cognitive development, so that he was using the correct wording to clearly express unhappiness and longing. That night we felt like opening a bottle of champagne to celebrate the latest milestone for our six-year-old boy! I would have loved to have run around the house naked shouting, *"EUREKA!"*

When your mum told you that the baby was sleeping next door, you my son went over there and checked if she was actually in her cot. After that, you calmed down and started to deal with it. It's incredible how your mind started to connect the different dependencies and correlations.

Another amazing moment to add to our list. I'm sure there will be more.

HOPELESSNESS

In the lives of every parent, there are days of hopelessness. More than once I've wondered what i could do to change your world, my son.

Feelings of powerlessness are a constant companion, but in my opinion, it is important not to get stuck in this state. I feel helpless almost every day. When you cry, and i don't know why. When i see that you're not well, when you have a cold and when i can't find the cause. It's painful when i see that you want something, and i have no clue what you expect from me. I fall into despair because i have no idea how to help you. The sense of vulnerability pins my shoulders to the ground. Many times, I have shouted with tears in my eyes: *"Son! Please tell me, show me, guide me! I want to help you!"*

I am a parent and i want to be better. I want to give you a piece of heaven on earth and i can't. It's such a sad experience. I know now that i have to take a note of every single one of your behaviours – writing down all the facts connected with the situation from start to finish, so that next time something happens i can quickly respond to your needs.

I am aware, my son, that there will be days when you will try to tell us something and we will not understand, and the sadness will break my heart. But you know what? I also want to catch those moments when you overcome an obstacle with success.

WHAT IS AHEAD OF US?

Beating, biting, pushing, and compulsive disorders – in Maks' case all these things turn up in trace amounts. We've reached a phase of constant screaming and disagreement with decisions we make. Almost every time we want something from you, Maks, your first reaction is to explode. I can't tell you anything, and i can't reprimand you. Sometimes even saying your name is enough. Wound as tight as a guitar string, you're like a live volcano, capable of blowing up at any minute. Sometimes i lack the patience to protect myself from the hot lava, which hurts me and your mum. Sometimes we're covered in ashes, my son.

I know that all of this is an outcome of your constant battle with emotion, your fight for independence, and your work in building your own character. We are trying as well. Fighting. Covered in ashes we stand in front of you with tears in our eyes. If i have trouble handling these emotions, what are you struggling with? I fear the day when i can't help you, when i won't know how to react to your behaviour. Most of all, I am afraid of the moment when i lack the skills and knowledge to help you.

A LITTLE BIT ABOUT US

Nikodem(Niko) and Ewa – almost like Adam and Eve, the difference being that Nikodem sounds better because it's a name worthy of an awesome guy. I'm being serious, but when i was a child i didn't like it. My brother's girlfriends were always saying how beautiful it was, but friends my own age used to wonder if it was even a real name. As i have mentioned, my childhood was happy but distinctive, unfolding in the playground, the bank and the post office. Split between parents, football and fights.

I was a fragile child. From the earliest age, my interest was in music and in rock bands. As an eleven-year-old i was wearing Guns'n'Roses T-shirts, beads, straps and peace symbols. At school, I wasn't too good, but i never failed and was always promoted to the next class. In primary school i usually got Cs, and later in high school, mainly Ds – but i always passed. I liked school, but i was too busy with poetry, music, philosophy and standing out from the crowd.

I was always different from the others – when other boys were playing football, I used to run away to 'hunt' in the forest. I loved trees, fields, flora, and fauna. My 'hunting' was, in fact, observing nature through binoculars, picking wild mushrooms and enjoying the beauty of what i could see. At the age of twelve or thirteen, I learned how to play the guitar, and thanks to this i found group of friends fairly quickly in high school. We put a band together. I was in my element: writing lyrics, singing and playing. Drugs and alcohol followed. Cigarettes were never for me, but any substance which expanded my imagination – definitely yes.

I was a young man from tiny town and i didn't at all fit into my surroundings. I went around half of Europe just by hitch-hiking, and i saw the whole of Poland from end to the end. Even when i had money, I choose to hitch-hike. I had the chance to try every possible form of transport, including an ambulance, a dustbin lorry, a police car and even a hearse with two dead bodies in it.

I love adventure and i love people. I'm positive, smiley, and i love being around people who are the same.

My wife, Ewa. a Highland girl from Nowy Sacz county. a fantastic woman and a fantastic mother. An amazing friend, and my best mate. We can talk about everything, enjoy each other company or just stay quiet together. She changed from a teenage girl into a real woman in front of my eyes. She has amazing style and financial awareness. In many areas, she is my teacher. We both love playing with fashion, and we both come from poor families where sometimes things were tough. She made me a better man. a beautiful woman who knows me through and through. After all this time, I know that i would be in deep shit if not for her.

She gave me four brothers-in-law, an amazing mother-in-law and a huge amount of incredible moments. I love her more than anything. Dark places have always been very tempting for me...rock'n'roll, devils, Satan. But when i go into the darkness, my wife lights up the road for me. She is my support, pushing me forward – and my successes boost her energy. We excite each other and have each other's backs. Beautiful.

DAUGHTER AND SISTER

Livia. Not quite four years old, with the energy of three grown-ups. When you were born, we were as happy as we were two years earlier when your brother came into the world. You were so small – tiny. You were smiling from the first weeks of your life.

Maks' world was turned upside down when we brought you home. He didn't know what was happening and he cried, unable to deal with the fact that he didn't have mum and dad to himself any more. His mind wasn't prepared for such a massive change – he didn't want to be anywhere close to you, but he didn't want to let go of mum.

The first year was a real nightmare for him. His development stopped, and i was under the impression that he was depressed. Kids, especially autistic ones, can have a tendency towards that. It was a difficult time for us as well since we had got Maks' diagnosis a few months before your birth. After that first rush of happiness came fear and sadness, that you might also have development issues. Luckily, you are amazing and full of energy – a big hearted girl who understands a lot and who takes care of her brother.

I was amazed when you started to take care of him when you were three – maybe even two. Everything always had to be equal – you used to ask me, *"what about Maks?"*. He also needed to get a piece of chocolate or a snack. Despite the fact that always used to push you away and didn't want to play with you, you were always by his side.

Of course, in many situations we couldn't avoid tears, fights and toys grabbed from each other – that's how things work with siblings. It took two years for Maks to accept your existence, but now he calls you *"baby".*

I think we divide our duties between the two of you pretty well and find the differences between your needs. We know that you need completely different kinds of stimulation to Maks, and that there's a risk of your childhood unfolding in the shadow of your brother's disability. I really hope we manage to avoid this.

You are a happy child with a big heart, and we are happy that you're starting to understand that your brother is a little bit different from you. I am sure that you will understand autism as well as your dad came to know how to live in a world of deaf people. You are fluent in both English and Polish. My beloved daughter, you are a surprise to us every day. One day, I would love to hear how you saw everything, and how you felt going through it with us. It will be a subject for another great book.

Be yourself, become whoever you want to be, and smile a lot. Your parents love you very much. You and Maks will always be the most precious and important things in the world for us.

FUCK–UPS, MISTAKES AND BAD CALLS

Well... Where should i start? I would like to share a piece of my story with you, so you don't think i am more resilient than i am. The kind of boy who got everything from his parents and was destined for greatness. In fact, I was destined to be average. No matter which way i chose, to a smaller or larger extent all roads led me into trouble. I couldn't focus on one particular task, and i had to act on every possible situation.

When i was fifteen i was writing song lyrics, poetry and composing music. In high school, I directed a dramatic play inspired by the music of Jim Morrison and The Doors and the philosophy of Friedrich Nietzsche. Added to the mix were alcohol and other perception-expanding substances. They kicked me out of one college, then a second, and after that a technical college, and then yet another place. Surprisingly, by the age of eighteen, I had only managed to finish high school. There were fights with my parents and brother. I blew up!

To cut a long story short, before i had turned seventeen i could tick off from my list several bands, hundreds of heavy drug parties, running away from home, detox in hospital, and rehab in a mental institution. Living away from home, some lovely people took care of me in Czaplinek. In Warsaw, I was fed by strangers, and over time they became my family. For almost a year, I ran a pub for a friend in small village called Malkinia Gorna, around halfway between Warsaw and Bialystok.

After all those adventures i decided to pull myself together and i finished college. Even in this reality i couldn't find myself, and i felt judged and pushed away. After some failed relationships, I decided to pack up my life and movc to London. I was twenty-three years old.

I made loads of mistakes, and many times i managed to fuck up completely. They say there's no limit to the number of times you can fuck up, but it's not important how many times you fail – what matters is how quickly you get up, shake off and move on. I've always fought, and today I'm not ashamed of any of it.

Maybe one day I'll write a book about the life of a kid who saw some remarkable times as a teenager: a life of adventure, acid, detox and rehab. I know I'm repeating myself, but this is only so i can get across the fact that I'm writing without any shame. I want to show that it doesn't matter how deep in shit you are, you can always start over. I'm a good example of it. There's a quote i like: *"Always and everywhere, you can do everything"*. I am living proof.

I'm not a businessman and I'm not rich, but these are not measures of success. I have an amazing family, I reach goals i set for myself and i push forward against all the odds. The only things that count are my family and my idea of fixing the world – enlightening people that disability and mental illnesses can touch us and those closest to us at any point in life. I wouldn't want anyone to go through the same, but if it happens, let me reassure you that even troubles and bad things can become an inspiration. Fight!

WHAT NEXT?

I set myself next goals and i want to continue my education. I am now working towards an open studies BA Childhood and Youth Studies degree through a Scottish university. During lectures, we cover everything related to childhood and growing up. We also discuss different aspects of child psychology and upbringing, and we analyse factors which have an impact on the behaviour of children and how they see the world of grown-ups.

My next dream, the target I'm working on now, is to become a specialist in picture communication. As I've mentioned, I would love to complete my training in PECS. I also want to continue writing my blog, and i currently post every few days. I use it to describe my feelings and share my thoughts after living through the process of becoming aware of autism. I write about all of the sad and happy stories from our everyday battles. I share all of it, so every reader visiting my blog can know that they are not alone.

All around the world, there are thousands of parents going through the same thing. It's good to know there is someone else with the same fears, feeling the same pain and happiness. I have received emails from Belgium, Australia, Germany, and the USA, strengthening belief in my work. Maybe it doesn't deserve the title of '*blog of the year*' but for me, it's a way of re-examining my emotions, tracking Maks' progress and sharing what's important with people. You could call it a kind of emotional exhibitionism, but for me, there is a method in my madness. It's my solution for staying in good health.

I love writing – that's why this book exists. Maybe it will never see the light of day, but how can i become a better writer and man – someone who can lift other people with good advice – if I'm not able to share my feelings?

The last two years have seen a series of successes for Maks and I, which gives me incredible motivation. In 2014, Edinburgh College named me Student of the Year, and i won a Scottish Qualifications Authority (SQA) Highly Commended award in the field of children's education. The SQA control standards of teaching and education institutions in Scotland, as well as being responsible for setting the education system's exam and work qualification benchmarks. Their Highly Commended award is granted to students chosen by college lecturers from around the country and is an extraordinary recognition. I will only add that in 2014, there were only a handful of awards given to foreign students.

In all honesty, it was all very special and surprising, because i am over thirty and i am a man, a combination not seen too often in early age education. Additionally, I have loads of tattoos and a rock'n'roll outlook, visible in the way i dress and in the way i am. This might make me stand out from a crowd, but clearly, it doesn't disqualify me.

I am proud of my achievements. Is there any reason i shouldn't be? All the results are the outcome of my strong will and hard work. In moments of doubt and struggle, I look at you Maks, my son, and use you as my role model. There are good and bad days, but you're always fighting, and you never give up. What sort of man would i be if i expected all of this from you and gave up myself at the first sign of trouble?

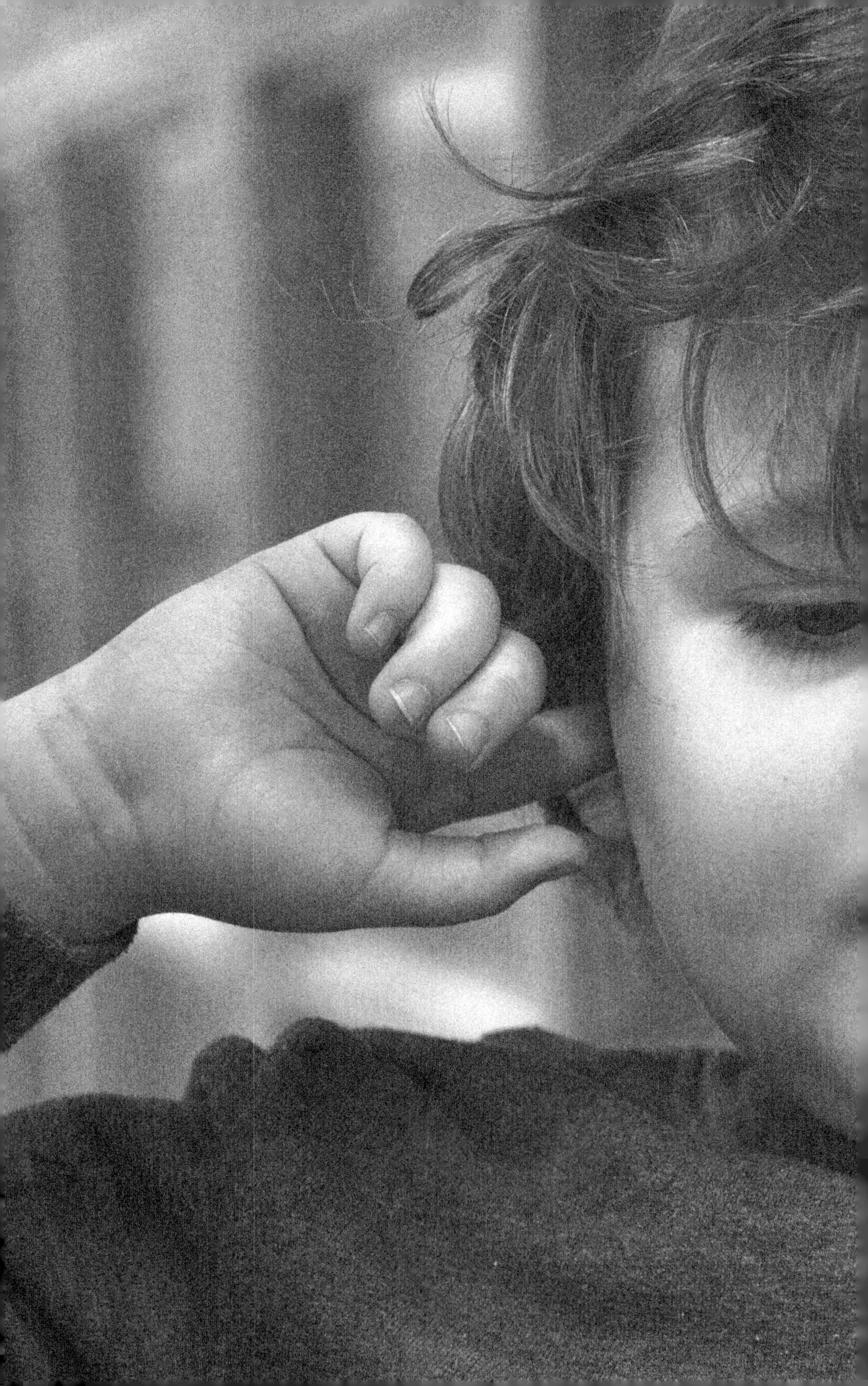

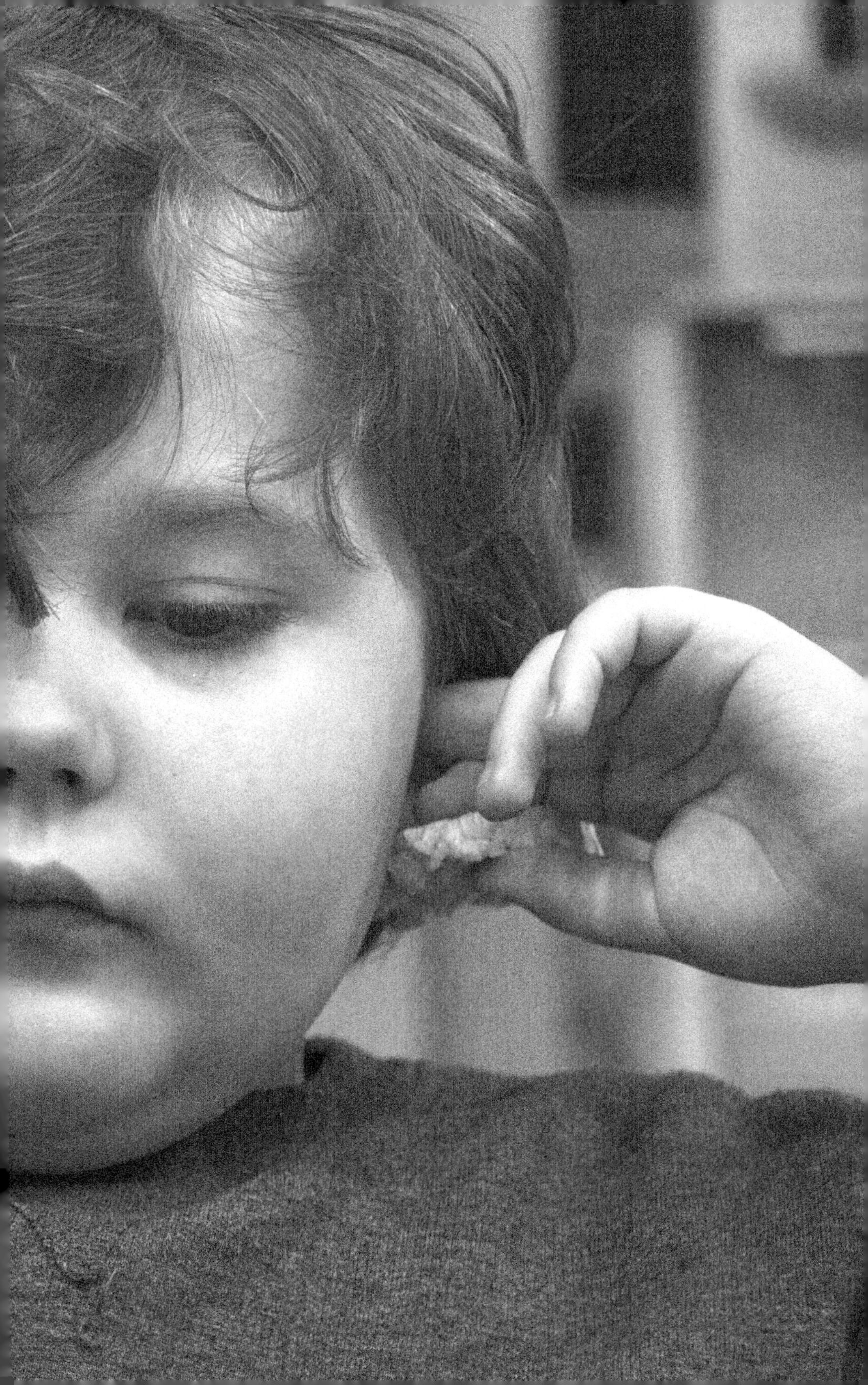

LIFE AS a CHALLENGE

What do i expect from life? That every new day will bring us fresh challenges and battles. I know that it will often be too much for us, and that sometimes it will be too heavy to bear – especially in moments of helplessness, when our son is suffering, and we don't know why, or what to do, or how to help him.

I would love him to enjoy good health. Since last year, I've been trying to eat cleanly and healthily, and now, lifting weights and building muscle, I've lost over 15 kilograms (2.3 stone). I actually enjoy it a lot and it gives me lots of energy. I'm look forward to being able to fight more stereotypes and push through more boundaries. Most of all, I never look backward, and i don't care about what other people say about me.

In the distant past, I took things people said and thought personally, but i didn't benefit from it. After all my teenage exploits, there was an overwhelming sense of having something to prove, a need to achieve something and become someone. a few years ago, when i stopped caring about what people say, I forgot about it all, and moved forward.

Today as i write these words, I realise how much i have achieved and how much more is still waiting to be done. But you know what? I don't have anything to prove to anyone, and i don't have to shout, *"Look at me! I made it!"* I don't care anymore; it is not a measure of my success. You can also think whatever you want about self-development and i won't try to change your mind about it, because i don't care about that either. I am learning, reading, progressing, educating others around me and i feel alive.

As a young man, I promised myself that i wouldn't want to live an average life: school, work, kids, mortgage, partying on weekends and so on – every week, month and year for the rest of my life. I want to absorb what world has to give, take my time, and be inspired by travel, cuisine, and life. I want to be an inspiration for others. I've broken the ugly stereotype of the Polish guy in Britain through education, awards, and recognition. I've broken the stereotype of being male and in early age education. I want to be a positive role model for all children.

With my life experience, education, and individual approach to life, together with my tattoos and piercings, I aim to be a rock for kids and their parents. I want to pay back the local community for everything they have given me over the last ten years. My wish is to change world – and if, thanks to this book and my work, just one person knows more about autism and disability, I can say it was worth it.

A few days ago, I was thinking back to when i was a teenager – somewhere at the end of secondary school. I used to make regular trips to charity shops and raid an old wardrobe of forgotten clothes at home, using an old sewing machine or my mothers' sewing kit to make alterations to trousers and the long collars of 1970s jackets. All to have original, outstanding clothes. Those days, one of my childhood dream was to be a fashion designer. I wasn't thinking about worldwide success, but quite honestly, even the stuff you find in shops now is pretty poor.

With support from my wife, I've decided to buy a sewing machine, and I'm going to learn how to sew properly and create my own designs. I hope that it will be another dream of mine which will start to take shape and become reality. I do know for sure that I'll never give up. My son never does. And who knows – maybe one day you'll hear about a clothing brand designed by the father of an autistic boy?

INSPIRATIONS

Working with people on different parts of the autistic spectrum allows me to understand more. I look at ASD as something individual which can affect everyone differently – you could say in a 'custom' way. Plenty of things still surprise me, but I'm not as shocked by some of these as i was some time ago.

My approach to life has changed. I observe people on the street and notice those who can't find their place in the world and in society. I always look at them with kindness. I can look at a person and see the story of his or her life without judgement – their own real story, not the fake one that society sees.

I am glad that my sensitivity has become different, that I'm open to new inspiration, that i hold on to my plans, and that i chase my dreams. I'm also happy that i can provide the impulse or spark for someone. If you have a need to talk with someone, please be my guest. Look on the internet for parents' websites – there's plenty of them. Even if you don't have the courage to write and share your emotions, fears, and stories with other people, you can always read. This way, I found a lot of amazing parents around me.

I'm an exhibitionist type of person, and i love to tell people what is happening in our lives. I have accounts on Facebook, Instagram, and Snapchat, plus my own channel on YouTube. I'm trying to build a brand, a sort of virtual business card for ASD, and all of it thanks to my son, who has been my guide on this journey. Because for me, autism is a journey, and although no-one ever told us it would be easy, we love our guide.

Very often i look at other blogs, simply because i love the progress of other kids. I feel like we are all creating unity, with each of us adding a little brick to a sort of house of common consciousness. Every sentence, photo, hashtag, or comment is an invitation to open discussion, and stick another pin on that big online map. To every question about autism from someone i know, or don't, I respond with a big smile. To those who are negative, I give down to earth answers injected with perspective – I don't take part in stupid, pointless conversations. I don't poke people in the eye, but i try to not get upset with them either. It wasn't always like this, but i am learning.

I could list so many websites which inspire me, not only concerning autism, but also those covering different ways of helping each other – sharing joy and happiness when the world around us is collapsing.

There are plenty of great parents in the world fighting for their kids, trying to make others understand that it's not disabled people who need to adjust, but them. We are born with the same rights; therefore, we have the same rights when we grow up. It's guaranteed by the UN Convention of the Rights of the Child and The Human Rights Act.

Sadly, I'm quite often under the impression that disabled people are expected to adjust themselves to others. Isn't that the wrong approach? In Poland, parents of kids with special needs are tilting at windmills because of the poor education system, the lack of access to medications and therapy, and the long waiting lists for those that are available. All of these factors contribute to people being sidelined – existing as living proof of broken human rights, stripped of their humanity and dignity.

THANK YOU, MY SON

I would like to say thank you to you Maks, my son, for turning me into a better person. I am far from ideal, but mindful pursuit of self-development has given me a sense of forward motion. It's getting better and better every day. I can sit down, make myself a cup of coffee and smile. I'm happy to be a father, a husband, and an educator, someone who has enough time to write a book.

Many years ago, like most people, I looked at the world differently. But i learned empathy from my parents, since they lived in a completely different world and did everything in their power to give my brother and i a good life. I understand that now. Thank you, Mum and Dad!

At this moment, I can see how similar the paths of our lives have been. I understand how they felt when their youngest son couldn't find his place in the world, and when he tried to take his own life. Those worries are so close to me now. The uncertainty and fear that accompanied them all the time matches the feelings we have with two kids of our own by our sides.

I know that sometimes my parents didn't understand some of the things i wanted to tell them and share with the world, not only because of their disability, but also because deaf people can have more general problems with abstract thinking. This sort of insight makes me watch and pay closer attention to Maks and Livia. Everything is for them, and with them. Today i worry about my children, but i always find beauty and hope in them.

Thank you, Livia, for taking care of your brother and all the wise words from your good heart. You're not even four years old and you already know so much about life. Thank you for your sulks and your smiles every day.

Thank you Ewa, my ex-wife, for being with such a weirdo for almost ten years. Without you I couldn't have got to the place I am right now. I'm sure that life has many surprises in store for us, and I'm aware of all the threats which may come, but I believe that whatever happens to us we will still be standing. For our children – strong. .

Thank you, dear reader, for taking the time to read my book. I hope that, after all, I have managed to break down the stereotypes around autism. Let's try to listen those who can't speak, so we can see what's hiding inside them. Stop for a second and think about your life – are you doing your best? If only one person in the world is helped thanks to my book, if one human being changes his or her views or is given a good enough reason to live – it was worth writing and publishing.

After 11 years together, in 2017 Ewa and Niko decided to go separate ways. They are co-parenting and together looking after their children, facing challenges as co-parents and ex-couple. Children have now two homes and still two loving parents, who are trying to share their responsibilities equally. They remain in good relationship.

Printed in Great Britain
by Amazon

39513186R00119